SLAVE LIFE

IN

VIRGINIA

AND

KENTUCKY

LIBRARY OF SOUTHERN CIVILIZATION

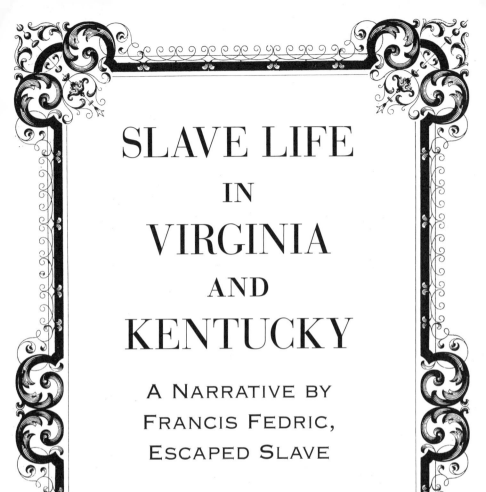

SLAVE LIFE
IN
VIRGINIA
AND
KENTUCKY

A NARRATIVE BY FRANCIS FEDRIC, ESCAPED SLAVE

Edited, with an Introduction and Notes,
by C. L. Innes

LOUISIANA STATE UNIVERSITY PRESS

BATON ROUGE

Published by Louisiana State University Press
Copyright © 2010 by Louisiana State University Press
All rights reserved
Manufactured in the United States of America
First printing

Designer: Laura Roubique Gleason
Typeface: Fournier MT
Printer and binder: McNaughton & Gunn

Library of Congress Cataloging-in-Publication Data

Frederick, Francis, ca. 1805–ca. 1882.
  Slave life in Virginia and Kentucky : a narrative by Francis Fedric, escaped slave / edited, with an introduction and notes, by C.L. Innes.
      p. cm. — (Library of Southern civilization)
  Includes bibliographical references and index.
  ISBN 978-0-8071-3683-6 (cloth : alk. paper) — ISBN 978-0-8071-3684-3 (paper : alk. paper) 1. Frederick, Francis, ca. 1805–ca. 1882. 2. Slaves—Virginia—Biography. 3. Slaves—Kentucky—Biography. 4. Fugitive slaves—Canada—Biography. 5. Slaves—Virginia—Social conditions—19th century. 6. Slaves—Kentucky—Social conditions—19th century. 7. Plantation life—Virginia—History—19th century. 8. Plantation life—Kentucky—History—19th century. 9. African Americans—Biography. 10. African Americans—England—Biography. I. Innes, Catherine Lynette. II. Title.
  E444.F85A3 2010
  975.5'03092—dc22
  [B]

2009051168

CONTENTS

ACKNOWLEDGMENTS

I am grateful to the Leverhulme Trust, whose financial support enabled travel to New York, Virginia, Kentucky, and Toronto, as well as frequent trips to the British Newspaper Library at Colindale in pursuit of Francis Fedric. Staff at the Schomburg Library in New York, the University Library in Toronto, and the Fauquier County Public Library in Warrenton, Virginia, gave generously of their time and assistance. I owe particular thanks to Jane Butler and Karen White at the Afro-American Historical Association of Fauquier County, in The Plains, Virginia, and to Lynn David and Cay Chamness at the Museum Center in Maysville, Kentucky, where I was fortunate to be given access to a file on Frederick compiled by Lynn David and Professor Randolph Runyon. In Toronto I was given many helpful leads by Dr. Afua Cooper, while Sara Salih provided hospitality, encouragement, and also, through her own work, models and inspiration for this enterprise. An anonymous reader for Louisiana State University Press provided many helpful suggestions that I was pleased to follow as best I could. I also thank Rand Dotson for his encouragement and the LSU Press editorial staff for detailed notes and corrections.

INTRODUCTION

FRANCIS FEDRIC'S STORY: HISTORICAL AND CULTURAL CONTEXTS

> Ohio's not the place for me,
> For I was much surprised
> To see so many of her sons
> In garments of disguise.
> Her name has gone out through the land,
> Free labor, soil, and men,
> But slaves had better far be hurled
> Into the lion's den.
> Fare ye well, Ohio, I am not safe in thee;
> I'll travel on to Canada, where colored men are free.
>
> —Antebellum African American song, quoted in
> Keith P. Griffler, *Front Line of Freedom*

In 1854, faced with the threat of yet another brutal beating, a fifty-year-old slave in Mason County, Kentucky, decided to make his second attempt to escape. His first attempt, about five years previously, had resulted in his near starvation as he hid for nine weeks in a swamp, before finally being compelled to return to his master. This time he sought the help of a neighbor with abolitionist sympathies, and he joined the hundreds of fugitive slaves who were smuggled across the Ohio River and north to Canada on the Underground Railroad. After his arrival in Toronto he discarded his master's surname (Parker), renamed himself Francis Fedric, and married an Englishwoman. In 1857 he traveled with his wife to the United Kingdom, where he lectured on behalf of the antislavery cause and published two versions of his life story. After the end of the American Civil War he returned to the United States, where, now known as the Reverend Francis Frederick, he published a third autobiography.

Born in Fauquier County, Virginia, around 1805,[1] Francis Fedric tells readers of his first published narrative that his mother's parents were brought from Africa to Maryland and then purchased by a man named Parker, for whose son his mother worked as a field hand. She bore nine children, two boys and seven girls, but Fedric makes no further mention of his brother and sisters until he tells of his escape from Kentucky and his grief at leaving them behind. Fauquier County records reveal at least three generations of Parkers who held several parcels of land in the region. Fedric's owners appear to be descended from a Dr. Alexander Parker, who had property in Bristol as well as Virginia. He had purchased land on the Walnut Branch of the Cedar Run river about twelve miles southeast of Warrenton (the county seat) in the northeast of Virginia, where he grew tobacco.[2] Upon his death in about 1800, his estate was left to his sons William and Richard, and his wife, Amy. Nearby was another larger plantation, owned by the Carter family, who are listed as owning over 200 slaves, one of whom was Fedric's father.

The tobacco which had proved a lucrative crop in the past gradually impoverished the Virginia soil, and during the nineteenth century some 200,000 white settlers moved across the Alleghenies in search of better land. In the process, approximately 40,000 slaves were transported from the Eastern Seaboard to Kentucky.[3] Sometime between 1815 and 1820, William and Richard Parker moved with their mother to Mason County, Kentucky. Fedric describes the long journey vividly, as the cavalcade of slaves trudged westward across the Allegheny Mountains, fearful of the towering rocks and wild animals such as wolves that howled at night. Once they reached Wheeling on the Ohio River, they traveled by boat to Maysville, which was to become the Mason county seat, and which is situated on the banks of the Ohio River. Another ex-slave and escapee to Canada, Josiah Henson, described following this route about five years later with twenty slaves, through Fauquier County, "over the mountains on the National Turnpike to Wheeling" and then by boat up the Ohio River.[4] In the 1820s, Maysville contained "a number of factories, a ropewalk, and a glassworks, as well as tobacco warehouses, inspection stations, and cigar-rolling plants, the last of which were usually staffed with enslaved women and children."[5]

The Parkers bought land some twenty miles southeast of Maysville. The field slaves cleared the uncultivated land of bush, fenced it, and sowed bluegrass seed for the cattle to graze. They also built log cabins for the new slaves that the Parkers intended to purchase at the slave market. Until 1833, when Kentucky introduced a nonimportation act, slaves were brought from the eastern and southern states to work on the new plantations in Kentucky. The act was repealed in 1849 to allow the purchase and selling of slaves down south, and several slave traders set up business in Lexington and Maysville, making profits of up to $150 on each slave sold in Natchez, Mississippi.[6]

Francis Fedric, however, was to become a house slave, and was trained to wait at table, cook, and take messages to neighboring ladies inviting them to call on his mistress. He managed to evade taking on laundering duties by ensuring that he tore any dresses he was given to wash, declaring that he was thus "sufficiently cunning by this stratagem to escape what appeared to me the degrading womanly occupation of washing."[7] Nevertheless, he seems to have been comparatively well treated by his mistress, and to have earned the reputation of being intelligent and trustworthy. He was eager to learn, and makes much of the gap between the brutalizing life of those working in the fields and the opportunities, however deliberately restricted, for those employed in the household to glimpse possibilities of a wider and more "cultivated" life.

Although his grandmother had been deeply religious (despite her husband's robust skepticism regarding the disparity between ethical behavior and the uses of the Bible made by slave owners who professed to be Christians), Francis in his youth shared his mother's indifference to religion. He was apparently about forty years old when he was first visited by a local woman evangelist whose interest and sympathy encouraged him in his desire to learn to read and to know more about the Bible as it might be interpreted by slaves like himself rather than by slave owners. Like Frederick Douglass, he is scathing about the hypocrisy of slave owners who profess to be Christians, and he castigates preachers who support slavery. Among the anecdotes he recounts concerning opposing readings of the Bible is the following:

I remember a slave, who was not treated very well with respect to food and other things, when he had done his work being lectured by his mistress on the duties of a slave, she telling him that in proportion to his obedience and servility as a slave he would be loved by God. One day, on receiving the Bible from his mistress, he began as follows,—"Give your slaves plenty of bread and meat, and plenty of hot biscuit in a morning, also be sure and give him three horns of whiskey a-day." "Come, come, stop that, Bob," his mistress cried; "none of your nonsense, Bob, there is nothing of that kind there." Bob, throwing down the book, said, "There, there, take it yourself, read it; you says a great deal more than you'll find there." (17)

Fedric's increasing interest in Christianity coincided with and also became the alleged cause for the brutal beatings inflicted on him by the son of Richard Parker, who inherited Fedric and other slaves after his father's death in 1847. According to Fedric, the son (Addison S. Parker)[8] was a dissolute gambler and drunkard, who became especially vicious when drunk, attacking household and field slaves with no provocation. Having suffered numerous assaults and threatened with a particularly harsh whipping after he had gone to a religious camp meeting without his master's permission, Fedric ran away for the first time, and hid in a swamp a few miles from the plantation. In the first two versions of his story he gives a graphic account of his hideout with its accompanying snakes and insects, his attempts to survive on berries and stolen morsels of food, and the desperate hunger that after nine weeks finally drove him to seek intercession from the Reverend Brush, who returned him to his master. As Leslie Howard Owens points out, swamps and caves were widely used hiding places by runaway slaves, and like Fedric, many, when their food ran out, "turned to stealing from local plantations."[9]

Back on the Parker plantation, Fedric found himself the object of even more frequent and brutal punishment. Around the fall of 1854, after a particularly harsh flogging, he decided he must try and escape to Canada, and sought the help of a neighboring planter who had abolitionist sympathies. Northern Kentucky, along the banks of the Ohio, contained many such sympathizers who took great risks to help slaves escape over the river. One was a former slaveholder named Thome, who had liberated his slaves, and would "get out of his bed in the middle of the night to help runaway slaves out of the reach of their masters, give them clothes and money, and sen[d] them across the Ohio river." Ann Hagedorn notes that between 1844 and 1864 forty-four men and women in Kentucky were convicted of the crime of helping runaways; some suffered severe beatings and privation in prison, and eight died in their cells.[10] An antislavery convention was held in Maysville in 1849. The Frankfort antislavery convention that met on April 25, 1849, included over 150 delegates from twenty-four counties, over half of whom, according to the *Presbyterian Herald* (May 5, 1849), were slaveholders. It also recorded that of the twenty-one ministers present, thirteen were Presbyterians.[11] Although none of the antislavery delegates were elected to the Kentucky Constitutional Convention held later that year, and the convention endorsed the "legal" existence of slavery, antislavery supporters continued to voice their opposition to the institution, and some gave assistance to runaway slaves. Horace Washington, who escaped to Canada from slavery in Mason County, and who had worked on a plantation almost next door to the Parkers, tells how he was helped to cross the river by a white man who "lived right in Maysville and sent others across by hundreds."[12] Fedric recounts how he was smuggled in a wagon to Maysville, where he was hidden in a garret for twenty-four hours, ferried over the Ohio River in the darkness of the night, and then conveyed from house to house along the Underground Railroad in Ohio.[13]

The crossing from Maysville to Ripley on the northern bank of the Ohio River was frequently used to ferry escaping slaves to the free state of Ohio. John Parker, himself an ex-slave who had escaped to Ohio in 1845 and purchased his freedom, bought a house in Ripley in 1849 and became a crucial figure in the abolitionist movement. He described Ripley as "the real terminus of the Underground Railroad," a place where blacks and whites worked together and with greater efficiency on the Underground than elsewhere, and a place where "every night of the year saw runaways, singly or in groups, making their way slyly to the country north." Parker made frequent journeys into Kentucky to escort escaping slaves and rowed them across the river.[14] Many of the fugitives were housed temporarily by the Reverend John Rankin, an ardent abolitionist, the lights of whose house on a hill above Ripley could be seen from the Kentucky bank of the Ohio River. Indeed, it was Rankin's house that gave refuge to the slave woman and child who escaped across the ice and became the inspiration for Eliza in *Uncle Tom's Cabin*.[15]

After the passing of the 1850 Fugitive Slave Act, which endorsed the capture and return to their masters of slaves who had escaped to the northern states, it became necessary to move escapees quickly on to Canada from Ripley. Fedric tells us that once he was across the Ohio River he was taken to a house outside the town and given some refreshment, a house that might have belonged to the Reverend Rankin or more likely one of the other abolitionists in the locality, such as Dr. James Campbell or Dr. Isaac Beck. That same night he was driven in a wagon accompanied by "eight or ten young men with revolvers" (86) about twenty miles north. His first overnight stop in Ohio might have been with the Reverend Gilliland in Red Oak, or slightly farther north in Russellville with Martha Lucas or the Reverend Jesse Lockhart.[16]

From November 1854 until May 1855, Francis spent six months recuperating in a "safe house" in northern Ohio, where two children in the family taught him the alphabet and then how to read the first chapter of the Gospel of St. John. Fedric records with gratitude and wonder the kindness and sympathy with which he was greeted on his journey.

From the station in northern Ohio Fedric was taken to Sandusky, on the shores of Lake Erie, and finally via Lake Ontario to Toronto and freedom. Fergus M. Bordewich records the detail that one boat, the *Mayflower*, "transported fugitives from Sandusky, Ohio, to Amherstburg, in Canada, with such regularity that it became known as the 'abolition boat,'" and in 1854 was the scene of a dramatic escape by the ship's barber, an ex-slave, who upon recognizing his former master on board leaped onto another boat, and then across to a ferry bound across the Niagara River to Canada. Many of the fugitives crossed to Canada from Detroit, where there was an active and forceful vigilance committee headed by

George DeBaptiste. According to DeBaptiste, his committee sent 1,043 fugitives across to Canada between May 5, 1855, and January 1856. It is possible that Fedric was one of those fugitives. Writing in 1854, Benjamin Drew gives a total of about 1,000 for the black community in the city of Toronto.[17] But there was a much larger community of ex-slaves and free blacks who had settled in Ontario, many of whom had fled to Canada after the passing of the Fugitive Slave Bill. Estimates for the number of black people living in that province in the 1850s vary from 30,000 to 60,000,[18] and include the communities established in the Wilberforce settlement north of London, the Buxton project in Elgin (founded by the Reverend William King, a reformed slave owner from Louisiana), Hamilton, the Dawn colony near Chatham, and Windsor. Mary Ann Shadd, an activist and editor of a black-owned newspaper, estimated there were 35,000 people of African descent living in upper Canada in 1853, but some recent scholars have, on the basis of census figures, estimated that the black population in Canada in 1861 was just over 20,000. C. Peter Ripley, however, gives 40,000 as a more plausible number, "three-quarters of whom were fugitive slaves or their children and, therefore, beneficiaries of the underground railroad."[19]

In Windsor, Henry Bibb, who had escaped from Kentucky to Detroit in 1842 and moved to Canada after the passage of the Fugitive Slave Law, published the antislavery paper *The Voice of the Fugitive* in 1852–53. Disagreeing with Bibb's separatist policies, Mary Ann Shadd founded with Samuel Ringgold Ward an alternative paper, the *Provincial Freeman*, published first from Chatham and then from Toronto. Shadd continued to edit this paper after Ward's departure for England and then Jamaica. Her paper promoted integration and equality for black people, as well as temperance, moral reform, and black self-help.

The response of white residents in Canada to this influx of black immigrants was mixed: a contributor to one newspaper, *The Colonist*, declared that "fugitive slaves are by no means a desirable class of immigrants for Canada, especially when they come in great numbers." Other newspapers and church ministers condemned slavery but favored "gradual emancipation." However, George Brown, editor of the Toronto

Globe, was fiercely opposed to slavery and published numerous editorials and reports condemning the evils of the slave system. Brown was one of the founders, and the first and only president, of the Anti-Slavery Society of Canada (1851–57). At its first meeting in February 1851, the society stated its objectives were "to aid in the extinction of slavery all over the world," to educate the Canadian public on the evils of slavery, and to "manifest sympathy with Negro fugitives coming in to Canada."[20]

When Fedric reached Toronto, he was assisted and then employed by the Anti-Slavery Society, or perhaps by its sister organization, the Ladies Association in Aid of the Coloured Refugees, founded in April 1851. This organization gave direct aid to the fugitives in the form of food, money, and clothing. Fedric speaks of the destitute condition of the refugees he was engaged to look after: "Haggard and emaciated, from anxiety and want of rest, men and women presented a most deplorable picture" (90). Having himself been employed mainly as a house servant in Kentucky, he betrays a degree of class and color prejudice when he goes on to describe rather patronizingly the different kinds of fugitive slaves he encountered: "Some of them were mulattoes and quadroons, and, being employed generally in household duties, they were very intelligent, and, in many cases, except to a practised eye, they could scarcely be distinguished from the pure white. Others were of coal-black colour, and, having been degraded to the uttermost, by abuse and hardship on the plantations, seemed but little removed from an animal; but a short period of kindness and attention, and freedom, seemed to work wonders in the development of their minds" (90–91).

While living in Toronto, Fedric met and married a British woman, a widowed immigrant from Devon. I have not been able to confirm her identity, but it is possible that she was the Jane Flynn whose marriage to a Mr. Francis Frederick on April 22, 1856, at the Wesleyan Methodist Chapel on Elm Street is recorded in the *Christian Guardian*.[21] An analysis by Barry Noonan of black residents recorded in the 1861 census for Toronto reveals that the majority were members of the Wesleyan Methodist Church, and also that marriages between black men and white women (from Ireland and England) were not uncommon.[22] In his first two narratives, Fedric announces his marriage proudly as a sign of the absence of racial prejudice among the English.

While in Ontario, Fedric also began his career as a lecturer, telling schoolchildren and factory workers, among others, about his experience as a slave. When his wife decided that she would like to return to England and join her family in Plymouth, the Anti-Slavery Society agreed to send him, carrying numerous testimonials from society members, including Corresponding Secretary Thomas Henning and the Reverend T. S. Ellerby. Francis and his wife arrived in Liverpool on August 27, 1857, and settled for a while in Plymouth. Shortly afterwards he embarked on a series of lecture tours describing his experiences and denouncing slavery in the American South.[23] A minister of the Presbyterian Chapel in Plymouth, W. R. Noble, testifies to the effectiveness and style of his lectures, declaring that "his public lectures are *speaking facts* rather than prepared lectures, and are both interesting and calculated to awaken sympathy in behalf of the victims of Slavery" (his emphasis).

The Reverend Noble's testimony is appended to Fedric's first known publication, *Life and Sufferings of Francis Fedric, While in Slavery*, which appeared as a small twelve-page pamphlet, published in Birmingham in 1859. It is republished here as an appendix to his later and much longer narrative, *Life as a Slave in Virginia and Kentucky*. Expanding on the "speaking facts" recounted in his lectures, the pamphlet was presumably sold after these lectures and at other antislavery meetings. Two years after its publication, it was mentioned in a Dundee newspaper:

Lecture by a Fugitive Slave

—It will be seen from advertisements that a lecture is to be delivered to-morrow evening by Francis Fedric, an escaped slave, in which he is to give some details of his escape from which he was subjected in the Southern States of America. Mr Fedric has published a small pamphlet relating his sufferings during 51 years of slavery; and from this his story appears in such a light as to interest its readers while they feel shocked at the system.

The report goes on to quote a long section from the narrative, detailing one of the cruelest floggings and its effects, followed by Fedric's escape across the Ohio River. Describing the author's lecture delivered the previous evening (March 18, 1861) in Hawkhill, the newspaper comments how "in forcible and graphic language, he described some of the scenes which he himself had witnessed while a slave, detailing, in an interesting manner, his own personal experience as such, and the adventures and hardships he underwent while escaping from the Slave States."[24] That issue of the paper also contained a long editorial denouncing President Lincoln's March 5, 1861, address that appeared to endorse the Fugitive Slave Act.

A further report on March 22, 1861, in the same newspaper (the *Dundee, Perth, and Cupar Advertiser*) is worth reproducing in full, as it allows us to see the intense popular interest in Fedric and what he had to tell, as well as shedding light on the economic benefits, however limited, Fedric derived from his lectures:

Lecture by a Fugitive Slave

—Mr Francis Fedric, a fugitive slave, held a meeting on Wednesday evening, in Castle Street Chapel, at which he gave an interesting account of his own experience of the evils of American Slavery, and his escape five years ago from the horrors of that iniquitous system. The Chapel was crowded long before the hour of meeting (8 o'clock), and many had to forgo the pleasure of hearing Mr Fedric for want even of standing room, for all the passages were cram-full. George Rough, Esq.[25] who occupied the chair, stated in a few words that the object Mr Fedric had in coming to Scotland was to raise funds to enable him to open a temperance Coffeehouse in Bristol—that he had already obtained L.100.10, and that as soon as L.150 was raised he would begin business in that line. Those who had not an opportunity of hearing Mr Fedric on Wednesday evening will be grateful to hear that he intends holding another meeting on Friday (this) evening, in Ward Chapel. The collection in Castle Street Chapel which Mr Fedric received, without any deduction, amounted to L.5.18s. It is to be hoped that the friends of the poor trodden-down African race will come out in great numbers this evening, and help, by their contribution, an escaped slave, and now a disabled man, to begin a business by which to earn for himself, wife, and child, an honest livelihood.[26]

This report is revealing in a number of ways. Not only is it the first and only mention I have encountered in my research that Francis and his wife had a child, but it also makes clear the widespread interest in such lectures by fugitive slaves, the linkage between the two causes of abolition and temperance, and also the ways in which Fedric was able to draw upon the wider significance of his individual experience in the past in order to secure his future. It is also worth noting that the report is a little unusual in that unlike other newspaper descriptions of speeches by ex-slaves during this period it makes no mention of Fedric's appearance or color.

In *Life as a Slave in Virginia and Kentucky*, Fedric tells us that since his arrival in Liverpool he had been "engaged in various parts of the country, speaking concerning my own experience and escape from slavery, and lecturing, as well as I could, about slavery generally." The 1861 census records Francis Fedric, a lecturer, staying in a boardinghouse in Stirling, Scotland, on April 7. The *Autobiography*, published in 1869 after his return to the United States, lists various towns in the United Kingdom where the author lectured, including Bristol, London, Birmingham, Manchester, Newcastle, Glasgow, Edinburgh, Aberdeen, Swansea, Dublin, and Belfast. His lecture tours follow a pattern well established by many African Americans who visited Britain and Ireland in the mid-nineteenth century seeking support for the abolition of slavery. Frederick Douglass, Charles and Sarah Remond, William Wells Brown, Josiah Henson, and William and Ellen Craft are among the better known of these speakers, and all of them drew large crowds wherever they went. But there were many others, several like Fedric and Samuel Ringgold Ward sent by the Canadian Anti-Slavery Society. Some of these speakers remained in Britain for a considerable time, and there were sufficient numbers in London in 1851 to form an association of "American Fugitive Slaves in the British

Metropolis," who held a meeting in London in August 1851 to commemorate West Indian emancipation.[27] William and Ellen Craft remained in Britain for nineteen years, undertaking a demanding lecturing schedule in Scotland and England soon after their arrival in 1850. William Allen, a classics professor who in 1853 had escaped from a lynch mob in New York State after marrying one of his white students, taught elocution in Dublin for several years before setting up a school in Islington, London, in 1864. John Brown, another runaway slave from Georgia, settled in Bristol after his arrival there in 1850, told his story at antislavery meetings throughout the United Kingdom, and later dictated his story to Louis Chamerovzow, secretary of the British and Foreign Anti-Slavery Society.

The report in the *Dundee, Perth, and Cupar Advertiser* tells us that Fedric planned to set up a temperance coffeehouse in Bristol, and one can find in local Bristol and Glasgow newspapers in the early 1860s numerous advertisements for such establishments, though more often than coffeehouses it is boardinghouses or temperance hotels that are advertised. However, Fedric seems to have decided that it would be better to set up business in Manchester than Bristol and, in 1861 or 1862, became the proprietor of a boardinghouse there. (At about the same time William and Ellen Craft had planned to open a boardinghouse in London, using income collected at antislavery meetings, but according to R. J. M. Blackett, opposition from friends led them to give up this plan.[28])

But the boardinghouse did not prosper. Fedric and his supporters blamed its failure on "the Manchester distress," the severe economic depression suffered during what has become known as the Lancashire Cotton Famine, lasting from approximately 1861 till 1865. While some earlier historians laid the blame for the supposed lack of raw cotton on the blockade of southern ports during the Civil War, more recent historians have demonstrated that there had been overproduction of cotton in the 1850s and that in fact large supplies of raw cotton were held in Lancashire warehouses during this period as manufacturers hoped for a rise in prices. But the consequence was that by November 1862, three fifths of the labor force was unemployed, and in March 1863, riots broke out among workers angered by a reduction in relief.[29]

In 1865 Fedric returned to North America, traveling first to Canada and eventually to Baltimore, where he worked as a colporteur, selling religious pamphlets and books on behalf of a church organization. Fedric's first two narratives close elatedly with his marriage to an Englishwoman, a marriage he perceives as a demonstration of the lack of racial prejudice among the English. The third version of his memoir, the *Autobiography*, published after he became known as the Reverend Francis Frederick, makes no mention of this marriage. Indeed, the 1870 U.S. census records him as the Reverend Francis Fredericks, Minister of the Gospel, living in Baltimore City with Elizabeth Fredericks, a "mulatto," born in Maryland. Apart from the *Autobiography*, I have come across only one other very intriguing piece of evidence of his activities in the United States. This is a report dated August 3, 1868, which reveals that he traveled as a preacher through Kentucky and Tennessee, among other states, after his return. The report states that police in Frankfort, Kentucky, had gone to the aid of "a Negro preacher, Francis Frederick, attacked by a mob of Negroes, in Frankfort, who bruised, beat, choked, and would have killed him. The police rescued him and lodged him in jail for protection. He is an intelligent and earnest missionary, well accredited, on his way to preach in Tennessee, and had preached very acceptably in Frankfort until a report, with no other foundation than that he did not preach politics, was spread that he was a 'rebel.'"[30]

Francis and Elizabeth Fredericks (or Frederick) can be found at the same addresses in Baltimore city directories for several years up until 1882. I have been unable to find any further trace of Francis Frederick after 1882, and I assume he died soon after. The absence of any reference to his English wife in his final autobiographical work is puzzling. A thorough check of records and archives in the United Kingdom reveals no death or burial record for a Mrs. Fedric or Frederick who was married to this particular Francis. Nor is there a record of the child mentioned in the Dundee newspaper quoted above. It is possible that his wife's death went unrecorded and was in part the reason for Fedric's decision to leave England, and also that Fedric felt it more politic for personal and political reasons once he had returned to the United States not to mention his former marriage to a white Englishwoman. Another possibility may be that his English wife left him and reverted to her maiden name, and that the child mentioned was her child by her previous marriage. If this were the case, Francis may have believed the ending of this marriage best be forgotten and erased from the record of his life.

AFRICAN AMERICAN SPEAKERS IN BRITAIN AND IRELAND IN THE 1850S

When Samuel Ringgold Ward visited Britain in 1853, he commented on the helpful impact of Harriet Beecher Stowe's *Uncle Tom's Cabin*, which was by then "in everybody's hands and heart." Stowe's novel, Ward declared, "had so impressed the antislavery people of the aristocratic classes, as to lead to the celebrated address of English women to the women of America, in behalf of the enslaved classes." This book together with the address it inspired, and Harriet Beecher Stowe's visit to the United Kingdom, according to Ward "awakened more attention to the anti-slavery cause in England, in 1853, than had existed since the agitation of the emancipation question in 1832."[31] It is in this context that dozens of African Americans toured Britain and Ireland in the 1850s and early 1860s speaking on behalf of those who remained enslaved in the United States.

As Blackett points out, however, the lectures and published narratives of African Americans who visited Britain before 1852, and their enormous popularity, had already paved the way for *Uncle Tom's Cabin*. As a result of emigration and intermarriage, London's black population, reckoned at about 20,000 at the end of the eighteenth century, had become almost imperceptible, although a few blacks remained visible as servants. But the early nineteenth century saw a small number of African American students and fugitives coming to Britain, a trickle that increased greatly in volume after 1850, to such an extent that they formed the self-help association mentioned previously, American Fugitive Slaves in the British Metropolis. Thousands of English and Scots men and women of all classes had flocked to hear Frederick Douglass on his 1845 tour of Britain, and within six months, his narrative had sold 4,500 copies. Moses Roper, who came to Britain in 1835, calculated that by 1844 he had given about 2,000 lectures and that his *Narrative of the Adventures and Escape of Moses Roper from American Slavery*, first published in 1837, had sold over 25,000 copies, with an additional 5,000 translated into Welsh.[32]

But after 1853, the fame of *Uncle Tom's Cabin* altered in complex ways the context in which visiting African Americans were received. Certainly it helped increase the interest and sympathy of British audiences, and more generally encouraged the growth of antislavery sentiment and co-operation with North American abolitionist movements. However, the extraordinary popularity of *Uncle Tom's Cabin*, or "Uncle Tom mania" as a London paper dubbed it, undoubtedly affected the ways in which African American lecturers and narratives were perceived and read, and per-haps also influenced the content and style of their lectures and publica-tions. Sarah Meer notes that between 1852 and 1855 not only were there over a million copies of Stowe's novel in circulation, including fifteen dif-ferent pirated editions, but there were also at least twenty different dra-matizations in London, as well as numerous Uncle Tom pantomimes and burlesques. Many Uncle Tom productions also appeared in provincial the-aters. Meer demonstrates the peculiar interaction between the traditions of blackface minstrel shows and Victorian melodrama in these dramatiza-tions, mixing sentimentality and righteousness, patriotic self-congratula-tion, the use of "exotic" spectacle and "Americanness," an episodic struc-ture, and a sprinkling of songs. Through such plays, "*Uncle Tom's Cabin* [was] made a useful cause for British self-congratulation, based on a pe-culiar image of America that was refracted and distorted by the conven-tions of melodrama." The characters, both white and black, were often caricatures, and the issues simplified. They exemplified, in Meer's view, a "dangerous ambiguity" with their "conjunctions of blackface and sen-timentality, patriotism and anti-slavery opinions."[33] Such productions, along with the enormous popularity of minstrel shows, many of which made direct reference to *Uncle Tom's Cabin*, contributed to what Freder-ick Douglass reported in 1859 as "an increase in racism in Britain since his first visit in 1845."[34]

At the same time, the interest in Harriet Beecher Stowe's novel and the attraction of minstrel shows nourished a desire to see and hear "the real thing." The appearance and accounts given by African American speakers were frequently tested against Stowe's version of slavery. Indeed, some speakers set the authority of their own experience against the lesser authenticity of Stowe's novel, as for example when the fugitive slave John Brown declares, "Mrs Stowe has told something about Slavery. I think she must know a great deal more than she has told. I know more than I dare to tell." Others were critical of her depiction of "good" slaveholders such as the Shelbys, while William Allen, a professor of classics hounded out of the United States after his marriage to a white student, was particularly incensed by Stowe's characterization of the "mulatto" George Harris and her banishment of him to Liberia. He commented in a letter to Frederick Douglass that Harris's conception of African nationality was "sheer nonsense," and Stowe should know that "nations worthy of the name are only produced by a fusion of races."[35]

The criterion of authenticity is suggested in some of the testimonials appended to Fedric's narratives: the Reverend W. R. Noble attests to the effectiveness of Fedric's public addresses as "speaking facts," while the report in the *Dundee Advertiser* quoted above describes how "in forcible and graphic language, he described some of the scenes which he himself had witnessed while a slave, detailing, in an interesting manner, his own personal experience as such, and the adventures and hardships he underwent while escaping from the Slave States." Here, as in other slave narratives, it is the testimony based on "personal experience," and indeed the absence of a formal lecture structure and style, which seems to impress the audience.

The slave narratives published in Britain and addressed to a British audience have much in common with narratives like those by Frederick Douglass, Henry Bibb, Josiah Henson, and Harriet Jacobs, first published in the United States. They similarly incorporate a declaration of place of birth, descriptions of a physically, emotionally, and intellectually deprived childhood, scenes of harsh brutality including vicious floggings, the selling and tearful parting of mothers and children, the sexual assaults on young female slaves, efforts made to learn to read and write, religious conversion, attempts to escape, and finally a successful and adventurous bid for freedom. But there are also differences in the British-oriented narratives that mark them as a distinct genre. Most were dictated or written as the end product of numerous lectures seeking to inform their audiences not only about the institution of slavery and its evils but also more generally about North American manners, customs, and geography. Moreover, these lectures were most often sponsored by ministers and religious groups. Thus the response to the particular interests and expectations of their audiences combines the genres of travel writing with antislavery polemic, conversion narrative, and autobiography. And like the Uncle Tom melodramas, they appeal to British patriotism and self-definition as "the land of the free" in contradistinction to the United States.

Fedric's first and second narratives demonstrate that process of shaping and reshaping a narrative within a British context, as well as the process of collaboration between the narrator and his scribe. The first, twelve-page version, *Life and Sufferings of Francis Fedric, While in Slavery,* is fiercely polemical, its tone set in the second sentence of the opening paragraph: "My father was a slave, and worked for a tyrant master of the name of Carter; my mother was also a slave, and worked for a tyrant master of the name of Parker."[36] Presented in just nine paragraphs, some of which extend breathlessly and with little punctuation over several pages, this pamphlet goes on, as the title page announces, to expose the "horrors of the slave system," and how it serves to waste "all cultivation of mind and manners . . . soil and . . . human labour" (100).[37] A large portion of this detailed narrative dwells on the scenery of West Virginia and Kentucky, and particularly on the nine weeks Fedric spent hiding in the Bear Wallow Swamp during his first attempted escape. Here Fedric's scribe devotes much attention to the "doleful cry" of the whippoorwill, the croaking of frogs, the blowing snake and other reptiles creeping over him, the howling wolves in the distance—details that make Fedric's hideout both distinctively American and replete with Gothic terror. At other times Fedric's desperation and emotions are conveyed with a syntax and rhetoric characteristic of the sentimental fiction of his time, as in this passage expressing his relief, fear, and confusion when at last a young slave girl brings him some bread, telling him also of the reward placed on his head and the threat of a thousand lashes when he is caught: "When she handed it over to me I felt how! what! I can scarcely say, I was so grateful. I have spoken of hunger, hunger was not now uppermost in my thoughts. The river, can I cross it? Shall I be able after all to get away? Shall I reach Canada, the land of the free? Shall I, can I, escape the thousand lashes? They will torment me unto death if I am caught" (105).

Such passages as these create a sense of a hybrid oral and literary genre, giving an impression of immediacy of expression together with the more poetic, or perhaps biblical, language of the final sentence. At times the inscribed narrator directly addresses his readers, as in his closing paragraphs, an appeal to an English sense of superiority over America, to religious sensibility, and to sympathy for the antislavery cause:

I cannot express my feelings at the kindness I have received since I landed in England from the English towards a coloured man, such is the difference between this country and America.

Reader, it is and ever will be my pride and delight to live a man of integrity, as becomes a christian in every deed. May it be said of me as of one of old, a christian in whom there was no guile:—

I have escaped through countless dangers,
From the man who claimed my soul,
Mind, and body as his chattel,
Subject to his control.

Now I have come across the British ocean,
Here in England is my home;
As to those who still in bondage,
Brethren unto thee I come.

(112)

Fedric's second memoir, published in 1863 and "taken down from his lips," includes many of the incidents and some of the information he had recorded in the 1859 narrative, but it is five times longer (nearly 30,000 words compared to just over 6,000) and differs significantly in tone and effect. Recorded and published in the hope of raising money and thus "obtain a livelihood," this narrative presents a much fuller and more rounded picture of Fedric himself and his development from childhood to young manhood to adult Christian, and finally a free and married man. While the gripping details in the first narrative of the journey to Kentucky and his escape and sojourn in the Bear Wallow Swamp are retained, much of this second memoir is taken up with anecdotes of slave life. The Reverend Charles Lee's preface refers to Fedric's depiction of "the sunny side" of slavery, and indeed many of the anecdotes are calculated to amuse his audience, as well as inform them. Lee's reading of Fedric's narrative as romantic, and sunny as well as dark, may well be influenced by his prior reading of *Uncle Tom's Cabin,* and we cannot tell whether Fedric's scribe also inflected or elaborated various aspects of the dictated memoir to accord with his own assumptions about what a book about American slavery should contain. I would guess that much of the information contained in chapter VIII about the produce and climate of Kentucky was supplied by Fedric's scribe from other (written) sources. The degree to which the language of enslaved African Americans is altered to accord with the "stage dialect" found in dramatized versions of *Uncle Tom's Cabin* and minstrel shows is difficult to discern. But undoubtedly the greater part of the narrative derives from "insider" knowledge, which includes references to people, places, and incidents that no Englishman could have been acquainted with, and a point of view that is often distinctively aligned with African American trickster strategies.

The earlier pamphlet sets out to expose the horrors of slavery and the sufferings of its victims; the 1863 narrative additionally dwells on the ingenious and determined methods of resistance, and the multitude of psychological defenses against the annihilation of their selfhood that the slaves employ. And whereas the first narrative begins with an emphasis on the tyranny of slaveholders and the obliteration of individual identity ("My father was a slave, and worked for a tyrant master of the name of Carter; my mother was also a slave, and worked for a tyrant master of the name of Parker"), *Slave Life in Virginia and Kentucky* starts by drawing attention to the stupidity of slaveholders contrasted with the superior awareness of their slaves. Thus Fedric tells of a slaveholder who believed that the sugar brought to him must be of inferior quality because it was cheaper than the last lot he had purchased, but was satisfied when the storekeeper sent him back the same sugar at double the price. Fedric concludes the story and its moral thus: "The Colonel looked first at the bill, and then at the sugar. 'Aye, this is something like; this is as it ought to be,' he said. I merely relate this anecdote to show what kind of persons the slave-owners, in some instances, are, and that the slaves are not always kept in subjection by a consciousness of their master's intellectual superiority, for the slaves often, behind their backs, laugh at their absurdities; but by a brutal system of terrorism practised upon them from their very birth" (10).

Fedric also reverses the usual representation of the slave as innately superstitious (for instance Jupiter in Edgar Allan Poe's "The Gold Bug"), when he portrays Colonel R terror stricken by a thunderstorm and cowering in his house surrounded by the five hundred slaves he has summoned in from the fields to protect him. In a precedent to Charles W. Chesnutt's "Goophered Grapevine" stories, he also tells how as a child he played upon the terror his master and mistress had of ghosts and goblins by producing ghostly laughter as he hid in a bush. "The slaveholders, as a body, are very superstitious," he comments (50).

These anecdotes illustrating the intellectual inferiority and gullibility of slaveholders are followed by examples of their moral inferiority and deviousness. Not only do they demonstrate their hypocrisy by claiming to be Christians while denying access to religion by their slaves, but they also indulge in rape, promiscuity, and drunkenness. *Slave Life in Virginia and Kentucky* appeals to its evangelistic temperance audiences through its emphasis on the drunken rages and consequent brutality and licentiousness of Fedric's second master. As does Douglass, Fedric argues that deliberate attempts by slaveholders to brutalize the slaves and make "the utmost difference between them and the white man" (14) more often result in the brutalization of the slaveholders and their families, so that even their wives and daughters enjoy the spectacle of sadistic floggings of naked male and female slaves, and sometimes take part in it. He also cites the example of a slaveholder who sold his own daughter, a quadroon, to a trader for $1,500.

In the light of such behavior, the questions raised by Fedric's grandfather, depicted as a powerful and respected man, 6 feet 4 inches in height, take on greater force. "How," he would say, "can Jesus be just, if He will allow such oppression and wrong? Don't the slaveholders justify their conduct by the Bible itself, and say, that it tells them to do so?" (16). His grandfather also physically resists his master when threatened with a beating, and the young Francis is forced to intervene to stop the fighting men from seriously hurting each other.

But Fedric also portrays other forms of resistance and subversion. In addition to the story quoted above of the young slave who reinterprets the Bible to command masters to give their slaves "plenty of bread and meat" along with "three horns of whiskey a-day," the narrator tells how he sabotaged laundry duties by deliberately tearing the dress he was given to wash, and persisted in milking the cow from the wrong side so that she would kick over and spill the milk. The youthful Francis shares with Olaudah Equiano the experience of at first believing that he is being watched by a portrait in the room where he is working, but whereas Equiano takes pride then and later in serving his master assiduously even after he discovers his mistake, Fedric feels justified in "going on strike": "When working within sight of the picture afterwards, I would say, 'I's not going to work. You don't know nothing. They don't give us nothing. I's not going to work for nothing.' And I did not half work, only just doing a little" (25). Fedric affirms what has now become the received wisdom of postcolonial theory regarding "sly civility" and "signifying": "Slaves are all of them full of this sly, artful, indirect way of conveying what they dare not speak out, and their humour is very often the medium of hinting wholesome truths. Is not cunning always the natural consequence of tyranny?" (17).

More than most narratives in this genre, Fedric's memoir attempts to present the voices of the plantation slaves and to give the sense of a communal life profoundly influenced by the system of slavery but not entirely

demarcated by it. While they are together, the conflictual but fond rela-
tionship between parents and children survives apart from and in opposition to the authority of the master and the identities as chattels that he
would like to impose, as exemplified by Fedric's anecdote of his childhood attempt to escape a flogging (from his grandmother) for hurting
another child, by pretending to be asleep. As he feigns loud snoring, the
women dispute whether he is actually asleep or not: "'He is not asleep.'
'But he is asleep.' 'He isn't asleep.' 'But, me tell you, he be asleep.' Thus
the women disputed. I thought I would help myself a little, and said, 'Yes,
I be asleep!' I forgot. But my uncle did not forget to take me out of the
straw, and to flog me well" (15).[38]

Fedric also dramatizes in detail the courtship and wedding of two
slaves named Fanny and Jerry, a description that does not escape some
condescension, sentimentality, and mockery but that nevertheless also affirms the genuineness of feeling between slave couples whom all too often
slaveholders would part by selling off to different traders. One might well
see these sympathetic and almost nostalgic depictions of the slave community as a function of Fedric's distance from them in time and space, and
his loss of such a community in Britain. But these representations may
also be a response to the characterizations and caricatures of black people
prevalent in British Uncle Tom dramatizations and minstrel shows.

Perhaps the fullest response to the blackface dramatizations and minstrel shows so prevalent in 1850s Britain is Fedric's chapter titled "The
Negroes Party," in which a group of slaves don the clothing of their masters and mistresses and mimic their manners and lifestyle. This is the
story of a relatively humane master, John Franklin, who pretends to his
housekeeper, Sookey, and overseer, Thomas, that he is leaving the area
for several months, but returns secretly, disguised as a beggar, to observe
what goes on in his supposed absence. He sees the slaves enjoying his best
food and liquor, dressed in their master's and mistress's finest clothes, and
hears long discussions of the good and bad qualities of various masters,
with a general agreement that slavery is to be deplored even under the
best of masters. In the end the beggar is recognized, Odysseuslike, by the
scar on his leg. Mr. Franklin later tells others "that he had been to a good

many theatres, but he never in his life was at one where he had so enjoyed himself as at the Niggers' Spree. He said if some of the women had had white faces, he should have thought it was their mistresses, their manners and demeanour being exact copies of the white ladies; and Sookey told me that Mr. Franklin said, 'Indeed, he never could have believed it if he had not seen it'" (60).

There are a number of ways in which this chapter might be read as a commentary on and reversal of the Uncle Tom and minstrel shows. One of the main characters is Thomas, referred to as Uncle Tommy by his wife, Sookey, and portrayed as a humane and respected member of the slave community, but treated with none of the sentimentality or condescension with which Harriet Beecher Stowe renders her Uncle Tom. Indeed, Thomas is both an overseer and manager of the estate, to whom, with Sookey, his master entrusts the "entire management of everything" (53) during his frequent absences of three to four months. In a reversal of power, it is Thomas who insists on treating the "old beggar" kindly and allowing him into the house, and who intervenes when some of the younger black women refuse to eat with him, in yet another inversion of racial power relations and behavior. It is an episode that effectively questions the racial categories and assumptions on which the minstrel shows were based, and demonstrates that it is class, wealth, and status that assign the power to give or withhold charity. Thus one of the older black women declares that the beggar should be fed in the kitchen and "should come to de table when we genfolks had done" (55). Moreover, the conversation at the dinner table is presented as a full, lively, intelligent, and sometimes sardonic discussion of the institution of slavery, the behavior of slave masters, and the aspirations of those who are enslaved, in a language that although marked as specifically belonging to varied generations of African Americans is nevertheless far removed from the stage dialect characteristic of minstrel shows. In its radical questioning of assumptions about racial inferiority, this particular episode compares with William Craft's *Running a Thousand Miles to Freedom*, in which Ellen Craft successfully masquerades as a white slave master while her husband performs being her slave.

Although the *Autobiography*, published under the name of Rev. Francis Frederick, includes much of the material contained in his first two memoirs, there are also significant differences. About one quarter the length of *Slave Life in Virginia and Kentucky*, it is addressed to an American rather than an English audience, and specifically "to the minds and understanding of those of his own race . . . that from its pages they may learn the great principles that will move them forward in the race of life." It also calls attention (in a rather perfunctory way) to the qualities of the sights and towns specific to the United Kingdom and Ireland, including an anecdote about the quaintly backward modes of travel in Ireland. The *Autobiography* retains, almost verbatim, the anecdotes about the "Negro Wedding" and the "Negroes Party" but avoids the polemical thrust of the first narrative and also expunges incidents emphasizing the stupidity or brutality of slave owners. In this version Fedric refrains from naming his former masters. Nor does he include the account of his nine-week ordeal hiding in the Bear Wallow Swamp. As the title suggests, the focus is largely on the narrator's own character and achievements, as well as his developing religious belief and vocation. This final memoir gives the impression of a written work, rather than a largely oral one transcribed, and lacks the vigor and telling detail that enliven the first and second narratives. Like the second narrative, however, it was probably written and published in the hope of making money, in this case to support Fedric's new wife and himself, and to fund his activities as an itinerant preacher.

Much of Francis Fedric's identity and history remains an enigma, even his name. The first two versions of his story are published in England under the name of Francis Fedric, and this is also the name recorded in the 1861 Scottish census and used for his lectures in Scotland. His third narrative, the *Autobiography of Rev. Francis Frederick, of Virginia*, was published in Baltimore in 1869. But for at least forty years he was probably known by his slave master's family name of Parker. His first two narratives (and the United Kingdom census of 1861) affirm that he was born in 1805 or 1806; his third publication declares that he was born in 1809. Even the authenticity and origin of his narratives have been questioned. The historian

John Blassingame asserts that *Slave Life in Virginia and Kentucky* (1863) is entirely fictional, a novel "composed by the Englishman Charles Lee," and this assertion has been reiterated without qualification or verification by Henry Louis Gates.[39] Neither Blassingame nor Gates, nor—as far as I can tell—any scholar other than R. J. M. Blackett seems to be aware of the first narrative published under Fedric's name;[40] nor has anyone noted that the author of the 1869 narrative is clearly the same person as the narrator of the 1859 and 1863 publications.

Speaking of fictional slave narratives, Blassingame wrote, "Frequently the novelists had their heroes engaging in practices almost totally foreign to slavery. The best example of this is the story of a fugitive slave written by the Englishman Charles Lee. In the story purportedly narrated by Francis Fedric, *Slave Life in Virginia and Kentucky* (1863), all of the slaves are chaste, cunning, and courageous. The reader begins to question the validity of the account when Lee records the slaves frequently shaking hands with slaveholders, talking about running off to Canada in the presence of their masters, using such expressions as 'fie' and 'bid you fare you well,' and offering high opinions of Great Britain and Englishmen." It is not the case that any of the three narratives "frequently" record slaves "shaking hands with slaveholders," while the expressions "fie" and "bid you, fare you well" appear only in the corn-husking episodes; those songs seem to combine elements of African work song and English ballad. One instance of slaves referring to escaping to Canada occurs when the slaves are not aware that the master is present in disguise; the other is in transcriptions of work songs on the plantation, where the owners may or may not have been present, but in any case were likely to have dismissed them as light-hearted songs rather than declarations of intent to escape. Nor do Fedric's descriptions of his fellow slaves as "chaste, cunning, and courageous" and his "high opinions of Great Britain and Englishmen" differ markedly from descriptions given in other slave narratives published in England during this period and before. Indeed, Fedric's first two narratives belong to a specific genre of autobiographies published during the mid-nineteenth century in England for a British readership, which seek support for abolition of slavery in the West Indies and the United States and which include *The History of Mary Prince* (1831), *A Narrative of the Adventure and Escape of Moses Roper, from American Slavery* (1837), John Brown's *Slave Life in Georgia* (1855), and William Craft's *Running a Thousand Miles for Freedom* (1860).

While it is indeed likely that parts of Fedric's verbal narrative (according to the Reverend Charles Lee "taken from his own lips") were embellished or rephrased by Lee or by Fedric's scribe, and while it is also likely that after so many years there were some chronological and other lapses of memory on Fedric's part, my research has shown that there are numerous precise references to places and people in Virginia and Kentucky that could not have been known to a clergyman living in England. These include the location of the Parker plantations on the Cedar Run in Virginia and in Mason County, confirmed by wills and land deeds in the Fauquier and Mason county courthouses. There are references also to ministers, slave owners, and fellow slaves whose names appear in slave schedules, wills, and other archival documents and newspaper records. Identifications of specific names and places appear in the annotations to the narrative.

Notes

1. The year 1805 is the birth date given in the 1861 census that located a Francis Fedric, Lecturer, in Stirling, Scotland.

2. See Fauquier County, Va., Deeds, 1759–1780, County Courthouse, Warrenton, Va., pp. 44, 56.

3. This number is given by Karolyn Smardz Frost in *I've Got a Home in Glory Land: A Lost Tale of the Underground Railroad* (New York: Farrar, Strauss & Giroux, 2007), 26.

4. Josiah Henson, *An Autobiography of Rev. Josiah Henson (Mrs. H. Beecher Stowe's "Uncle Tom")*, ed. J. Lobb (London: Christian Age, 1890), 39–41.

5. Frost, *I've Got a Home in Glory Land*, 27–8.

6. The 1833 Kentucky nonimportation act sought to prevent slaves from other states from being brought into Kentucky and sold at the markets, although the law was often ignored. Karolyn Smardz Frost cites a speech made in 1840 by Robert Wickcliffe, "the largest slaveholder in Kentucky," declaring that some 60,000 Kentucky slaves had been sold to the Deep South during the previous seven years (*I've Got a Home in Glory Land*, 40). According to J. Winston Coleman, the act was repealed in 1849 because farming in Kentucky had proved less profitable than selling slaves down south ("Lexington's Slave Dealers and Their Southern Trade," *Filson Club History Quarterly*, 12 [1938], 22).

7. Page 23 herein. Further page references will be inserted parenthetically in the text.

8. A will for Richard Parker was recorded in 1847, leaving all his slaves and property to his son, Addison S. Parker (Mason County Courthouse Records, Willbook O, 11–13).

9. Leslie Howard Owens, *This Species of Property: Slave Life and Culture in the Old South* (New York: Oxford University Press, 1976), 87–88.

10. Keith P. Griffler, *Front Line of Freedom: African Americans and the Forging of the Underground Railroad in the Ohio Valley* (Lexington: University Press of Kentucky, 2004), 97; Ann Hagedorn, *Beyond the River: The Untold Story of the Heroes of the Underground Railroad* (New York: Simon & Schuster, 2002), 254.

11. Lowell H. Harrison, *The Antislavery Movement in Kentucky* (Lexington: University Press of Kentucky, 1978), 57. See Harrison for further information about the nature of abolitionist and emancipationist movements in Kentucky.

12. Hagedorn, *Beyond the River*, 249.

13. Various versions of how the Underground Railroad got its name have been recounted. According to Wilbur Siebert, the name originated in 1831 when another Kentucky slave, Tice Davids, escaped by swimming across the Ohio River, and mysteriously disappeared. His owner, who had been close behind the escaping slave, exclaimed, "The d———d Abolitionists must have a rail road under the ground by which they run off n———" (Wilbur Siebert, *The Underground Railroad from Slavery to Freedom* [New York: Macmillan, 1898]). In *The Liberty Line: The Legend of the Underground Railroad* (Lexington: University of Kentucky Press, 1961), Larry Gara expresses skepticism about this and other anecdotes, pointing out that the same stories are recounted regarding incidents in Pennsylvania and elsewhere.

14. Hagedorn, *Beyond the River*, 233, 234ff. See also Stuart Seely Sprague, ed., *His Promised Land: The Autobiography of John P. Parker, Former Slave and Conductor on the Underground Railroad* (New York: Norton, 1996).

15. See Hagedorn, *Beyond the River*, 300 n.135.

16. For a detailed study of abolitionists assisting fugitive slaves during this period, see Hagedorn, *Beyond the River*, chaps. 26 and 27.

17. Fergus M. Bordewich, *Bound for Canaan: The Underground Railroad and the War for the Soul of America* (New York: Amistad, 2005), 256; C. Peter Ripley, ed., *The Black Abolitionist Papers, Vol. II: Canada, 1830–1865* (Chapel Hill: University of North Carolina Press, 1987), 21; Benjamin Drew, *The Refugee: North-Side View of Slavery* (1855; Reading, Mass.: Addison-Wesley, 1969), 65.

18. Drew, who records the testimony of more than one hundred ex-slaves, including Harriet Tubman, estimates that there were 30,000 "colored" people in upper Canada in 1852 (*The Refugee*, xxvii, 65). Fred Landon calculates that "from fifteen to twenty thousand Negroes entered Canada between 1850 and 1860, increasing the Negro population of the British provinces from about 40,000 to 60,000" ("The Negro Migration to Canada after the Passing of the Fugitive Slave Act," *Journal of Negro History* 5 [January 1920]: 22–36).

19. Bordewich, *Bound for Canaan,* 379; Ripley, *The Black Abolitionist Papers, Vol. II,* 21.

20. *The Colonist,* quoted in Ian Pemberton, "The Anti-Slavery Society of Canada" (M.A. thesis, University of Toronto, 1967), 33; *Anti-Slavery Society Constitution and By Laws* (Toronto, 1851).

21. *Christian Guardian,* April 30, 1856, 3. The officiating clergyman was the Reverend James Borland.

22. Barry Christopher Noonan, *Blacks in Canada, 1861* (Madison, Wisc.: B. Noonan, 2000). Noonan finds a total of 1,008 black people in Toronto and 17,149 for Ontario as a whole.

23. Local newspapers during this period (September 1857–end 1858) focused almost entirely on the events subsequently referred to as "the Indian Mutiny," including the Siege of Lucknow and Delhi, with lists of British soldiers killed in action. These events entirely eclipsed reporting of the lectures that Fedric and others may have given at this time, and so there appears to be no record of his activities in Devon and Cornwall apart from his own account and testimonies appended to his narratives.

24. *Dundee, Perth, and Cupar Advertiser,* March 19, 1861, 3.

25. George Rough, a member of the Benvie and Liff parochial board, identified himself at another meeting, reported in the same issue of the paper, as a "radical reformer"— i.e., a believer that men should have a voice in the selection of those who are to govern them but should also contribute according to their means to that government.

26. *Dundee, Perth, and Cupar Advertiser,* March 22, 1861, 3.

27. R. J. M. Blackett, ed., *Running a Thousand Miles for Freedom: The Escape of William and Ellen Craft from Slavery* (Baton Rouge: Louisiana State University Press, 1999), 64.

28. Ibid., 71.

29. In the late 1850s and early 1860s, abolitionists and cotton manufacturers in Britain advocated a boycott of cotton from the slave states and sought to encourage the production and importation of cotton from alternative sources, including India and West Africa. Such moves regarding West Africa were supported by African Americans such as Martin Delaney and Robert Campbell. In 1862 and then from 1863 till 1867, William Craft spent time in West Africa setting up a school in Whydah and trying to persuade the king of Dahomey to cease the "atrocities" he was rumored to sanction, and to permit the establishment of cotton plantations in the area. (See Blackett, *Running a Thousand Miles for Freedom,* 75–87.)

30. This news report was contained in a file on Fedric held at the Museum Center in Maysville, Kentucky. Unfortunately, the details of the original newspaper in which it appeared and the journal in which it was reprinted were not available, and I have not been able to trace them.

31. Samuel Ringgold Ward, *Autobiography of a Fugitive Negro: His Anti-Slavery Labours in the United States, Canada, and England* (London: John Snow, 1855), 248–9.

32. R. J. M. Blackett, *Building an Antislavery Wall: Black Americans in the Atlantic*

Abolitionist Movement, 1830–1860 (Baton Rouge: Louisiana State University Press, 1983), 26, 5.

33. Sarah Meer, *Uncle Tom Mania: Slavery, Minstrelsy, and Transatlantic Culture in the 1850s* (Athens: University of Georgia Press, 2005), 133–54; quotes on 134, 141, 158. See also Audrey Fisch, *American Slaves in Victorian England: Abolitionist Politics in Popular Literature and Culture* (Cambridge: Cambridge University Press, 2000), 11–32.

34. R. J. M. Blackett, "Cracks in the Anti-Slavery Wall," in *Liberating Sojourn: Frederick Douglass and Transatlantic Reform*, ed. Alan J. Rice and Martin Crawford (Athens: University of Georgia Press, 1999), 192.

35. John Brown, *Slave Life in Georgia: A Narrative of the Life, Sufferings, and Escape of John Brown, a Fugitive Slave, Now in England*, ed. L. A. Chamerovzow (London: W. M. Watts, 1855), 60; Allen, cited in Benjamin Quarles, *Black Abolitionists* (New York: Oxford University Press, 1969), 221.

36. See appendix, 99. Page references for subsequent quotations from *Life and Sufferings* will be given parenthetically in the text.

37. I have inserted additional paragraph breaks and punctuation in the version published here to make it more readable.

38. Compare the transcription of African American dialogue here and in the "Negroes Party" episodes with the representations in Fedric's *Autobiography*.

39. John W. Blassingame, *The Slave Community: Plantation Life in the Antebellum South* (New York: Oxford University Press, 1972), 233; Henry Louis Gates, Jr., "A Dangerous Literacy: The Legacy of Frederick Douglass," *New York Times Book Review*, May 28, 1995, 3.

40. Blackett includes a reference to Fedric's first narrative in a footnote to his excellent study of black antislavery activists in Britain, *Building an Antislavery Wall*, 29.

A NOTE ON THE TEXTS

Fedric's first memoir, *Life and Sufferings of Francis Fedric, While in Slavery: An Escaped Slave after 51 Years in Bondage*, was published as a twelve-page pamphlet by Tonks and Jones, Birmingham, in 1859. A report in the *Dundee, Perth, and Cupar Advertiser* (March 19, 1861) suggests that it was sold to members of the audience after Fedric's lectures at antislavery, religious, and temperance meetings. A copy, the only one that I have been able to locate, is held in the British Library in London, and it is bound together with ten other antislavery pamphlets into a volume titled *Tracts on Slavery, 1827–77.* The other pamphlets include two lectures by Thomas Clarkson translated into Spanish and Ralph Waldo Emerson's "Address Delivered in Concord, Massachusetts, on 1st August, 1844, on the Anniversary of the Emancipation of the Negroes in the British West Indies."

The second memoir, *Slave Life in Virginia and Kentucky; or, Fifty Years of Slavery in the Southern States of America*, was published in London as a separate book in 1863 by Wertheim, Macintosh and Hunt, who published Alexander Crummell's *The Negro Race Is Not Under a Curse* in the same year. As the preface by the Reverend Charles Lee makes clear, *Slave Life in Virginia and Kentucky* also was distributed and sold to secure a living for Fedric. The book was reviewed and recommended to readers in the *Caledonian Mercury* (Edinburgh, Scotland) on September 19, 1863, as a "harrowing tale" that would, it was hoped, "help many in this country to rid themselves of that un-British feeling that has too long lent itself to the iniquitous cause of the slave-holding South."

Fedric's third narrative, the *Autobiography of Rev. Francis Frederick, of Virginia*, was published in Baltimore in 1869. It is not reproduced in this volume because much of it merely duplicates sections from *Slave Life in Virginia and Kentucky*, and also because it is available electronically.

The second and third of Fedric's memoirs have been digitalized and published electronically by the University of North Carolina, as part of its project "Documenting the American South." *Slave Life in Virginia and Kentucky* can be accessed at www.docsouth.unc.edu/neh/fedric/menu.html; the *Autobiography* is available at www.docsouth.unc.edu/neh/frederick/menu.html. There are some minor differences between the digitalized versions of these memoirs and the printed ones. For the two memoirs reproduced in this volume, I have adopted the versions found in the original printed texts. The very few changes I have made to the printed texts were to correct occasional misspellings of names and places or typographical errors, and to alter punctuation where it was necessary to clarify the sense (particularly in the case of *Life and Sufferings of Francis Fedric*).

Since it is the longest and most detailed text, I have annotated most fully *Slave Life in Virginia and Kentucky*. *Life and Sufferings of Francis Fedric* is reprinted here as an appendix, to which I have provided annotations only where they seemed necessary and not a repetition of information already supplied by the main text or my commentary and notes for it.

SLAVE LIFE

IN

VIRGINIA AND KENTUCKY;

OR,

Fifty Years of Slavery

IN THE

SOUTHERN STATES OF AMERICA.

BY

FRANCIS FEDRIC,

AN ESCAPED SLAVE.

WITH PREFACE,

BY THE REV. CHARLES LEE, M.A.,

INCUMBENT OF HOLY TRINITY, HAVERSTOCK-HILL

PREFACE

The Memoir contained in the following pages may, I believe, be thoroughly relied on as both genuine and authentic. The Author, Francis Fedric, came to me well recommended; and, since he has been in London, has been continually under my notice. I have every reason to regard him (as his many friends represent him) as an honest man, and a good Christian. His testimonials are signed, amongst others, by the well-known names of Dr. Guthrie,[1] Dr. Alexander,[2] and Dr. Johnston,[3] of Edinburgh; by Samuel Gurney, Esq.,[4] of London; and by the Revs. C. J. Goodhart[5] and Gerald Blunt,[6] of Chelsea. His references also to ministers of religion,

1. Dr. Thomas Guthrie (1803–73) became parish minister and very popular preacher for St. John's Church in Edinburgh beginning in 1840. He edited the *Sunday Magazine* and published, among other works, *The Gospel in Ezekiel* and *Seedtime and Harvest* (1860), the latter containing his three pamphlets concerning ragged schools (schools for poor children). He founded three ragged schools in Edinburgh—one for boys, one for girls, and one for children under ten. In all, they catered to 265 children.

2. William Lindsay Alexander, D.D. (1808–84), was minister for the Augustine Church (now Augustine United Church), Edinburgh, from 1835 till 1877. He was a forceful advocate for the abolitionist campaign during the American Civil War.

3. Possibly the Rev. J. A. Johnston, one of the founders of the Scottish Temperance League, formed at Falkirk. He became president of the League, whose headquarters were in Glasgow, in 1872.

4. The Samuel Gurney mentioned here was the son of the Quaker banker and philanthropist Samuel Gurney who died in 1856, leaving Cranham Manor (then known as Ham Manor) and the running of his bank to his son. Samuel Gurney Sr. was an active member of the Anti-Slavery Society.

5. Probably a reference to the Reverend F. C. Goodhart, minister of Park Chapel in Chelsea, who lived in Grove House, in Hollywood Road, Chelsea, between 1853 and 1868 ("Little Chelsea in Kensington," *Survey of London*, vol. 41 [1983], www.british-history.ac.uk/report.aspx?compid=50021).

6. The Reverend Abel Gerald Wilson Blunt (1827–1902), a cousin of Wilfred Scawen

and others, by whom he was employed in Toronto, to look after escaped slaves, are completely satisfactory.[7]

The narrative itself will sufficiently disclose the sad tale of bondage and brutality, to which, for fifty years of his life,[8] poor Fedric was an unfortunate victim. Escaped from slavery, and finding his way to our own country, the encouragement and assistance of sympathizing friends enabled him to establish a lodging-house in Manchester. That blight of slavery, however, which had fallen so heavily on his previous life, still seemed to pursue him—originating the war between the North and the South (whether directly or indirectly need not now be discussed). This was immediately followed by the Manchester distress,[9] and Fedric at once lost

Blunt, was parish priest for St. Luke's Church in Chelsea from 1860 till 1902, and lived in the Old Rectory in Church Lane, Chelsea. He built a large soup kitchen onto the rectory in 1861 and founded a "working men's reading room" in 1862. In addition to Francis Fedric (perhaps a visitor to the reading room—or possibly the soup kitchen), his neighbors and acquaintances included Mrs. Gaskell, John Ruskin, the Wedgwoods, the Thackerays, Henry Kingsley, J. R. Froude, and the actor William Charles Macready. Thomas and Jane Carlyle were frequent visitors, and we are told that despite disliking Thomas Carlyle's dismissive attitude toward "other men of all kinds," Blunt appreciated his "greatness" (Reginald Blunt, *Memoirs of Gerald Blunt of Chelsea* [London: printed for the author, 1911]).

7. One of these referees was doubtless the Reverend T. S. Ellerby, whose letter of recommendation Fedric mentions in the final chapter of this narrative. A Reverend T. S. Ellerby was pastor of the First Congregational Church in John Street, Toronto, and is listed as a member of the Committee of the Anti-Slavery Society of Canada in its 1857 report.

8. The number of years Fedric spent in slavery is given as fifty-one in his earlier narrative (see appendix), and forty-six in his third autobiography, where Fedric gives his date of birth as 1809.

9. More commonly called the Lancashire Cotton Famine (1861–65). Lee's reference to a connection between slavery and "the Manchester distress" supposes, as several contemporary commentators and later historians maintained, that it was caused by federal ships blockading the ports of the southern states, preventing them from shipping raw cotton to the north of England. During this period many cotton mills in Lancashire closed, and by November 1862, over 300,000 men and women were out of work. Although some workers and mill owners were sympathetic to the Unionist cause and the abolition of slavery, others urged the British government to force President Lincoln to lift the blockade. Resentment at the miserable conditions and minimal charity offered led to riots in March 1863. (See W. O. Henderson, *The Lancashire Cotton Famine, 1861–1865* [Manchester: Manchester University Press, 1934]). Recent historians such as Eu-

the scanty subsistence he had relied on. Being paralyzed in his hands by exposure in the swamps, he is altogether unable to follow handiwork of any kind. He is, however, a very effective lecturer, and is fully capable of riveting the attention of an audience by the romantic details of his very interesting life. To help him a little to thus obtaining a livelihood, and hoping that, before long, by the aid of whatever funds he may realize, he will be able to re-establish himself in some kind of business, I have induced a gentleman of this neighbourhood to take down from his lips the memoir now given to the public. It presents no one-sided view of slavery; but the sunny side (if bondage has any bright side), as well as its darker and more hateful tints, are all fairly and truthfully depicted. When we think of quadroons, and the detestable secrets with which their career is shockingly and shamefully associated—when we think of the enforced separation of the poor slave from his wife, and of children from their parents, notwithstanding all that can possibly be said of kind and humane masters—when we add the liability of being sold at any time into the hands of some hardhearted man, it is impossible not to shudder at so accursed a system, and to pray God, in His own good time, and best way, to smite off every fetter and set the captives free.

Charles Lee, M.A.,[10]

Incumbent of Holy Trinity, Haverstock-hill.

8, Camden-square, London, N.W.,

Feb. 16, 1863.

---

gene Brady and Douglas Farnie have argued that with or without the American Civil War the Lancashire cotton industry would have suffered a depression in the early 1860s owing to massive overproduction and speculation in the late 1850s, and that merchants held large stocks of raw cotton in Lancashire during the Civil War hoping for a further rise in prices. When the Prince of Wales's marriage to the Danish princess Alexandra was celebrated, several cotton mills in Lancashire towns hoisted the Confederate flag in tribute. See D. A. Farnie, "The Cotton Famine in Great Britain," in B. M. Ratcliffe, ed., *Great Britain and Her World, 1750–1914: Essays in Honour of W. O. Henderson* (Manchester: Manchester University Press, 1975); E. A. Brady, "A Reconsideration of the Lancashire Cotton Famine," *Agricultural History* (July 1963): 156–62. See also R. J. M. Blackett, ed., *Running a Thousand Miles for Freedom: The Escape of William and Ellen Craft from Slavery* (Baton Rouge: Louisiana State University Press, 1999), 74–5.

10. The Reverend Charles Lee was the Vicar of Holy Trinity Church, Clarence Way, Haverstock Hill (Camden), from 1860 to 1871.

CONTENTS

CHAPTER I.

*Birth-place—Earliest Recollections—Slave Girl Flogged—Fear of a
Slaveholder during a Thunderstorm—Father and Mother—Piety of Grand-
mother, a Native African—Systematic Degradation of Slave Children—
Grandmother the first Person I saw Flogged—Feeding of Slaves—
Grandmother's Happy Death—Cunning of Slaves.*

I was born in Fauquier County, in Old Virginia. My remembrance, as
nearly as I can reckon, extends back to my eighth or ninth year of age.
Some little striking incidents occur, now and then to my mind, which
happened when I was somewhat younger even than that. My master's
house, a frame one, as it is called in America, was situated on a gently rising ground, skirted by a small stream, emptying itself into a deep rivulet, named the Cedar Run.[11] This rivulet was from twenty to thirty yards
wide, and during the rainy season dashed along at a headlong pace, carrying with it trees and logs, and overflowing very often large tracts of the
surrounding country, which was mostly of a level character. But although
near so fine a body of water, unlike most slaves, I never learned to swim,
which deficiency, as you will find in the sequel, was one of the greatest
misfortunes of my life.

Almost the first circumstance which I recollect is this. A Mrs. R——,
the wife of a Colonel R——,[12] who had a large plantation near to my

11. In *Life and Sufferings of Francis Fedric* (reproduced in the appendix), Fedric notes
that the property was "within nine miles of Cedar Run." The Cedar Run is a sizable
stream that runs from approximately 3 miles northeast to 15 miles south of Warrenton,
the county seat of Fauquier County, Virginia, and then turns east toward and into Prince
William County.

12. Possibly Colonel Thomas Jefferson Randolph, who according to the 1800 U.S.
census owned a plantation of 63,000 acres in Albemarle County, Virginia. Members of
the family, also possessing large numbers of slaves recorded in the 1850 slave schedules,

master's, possessing four or five hundred slaves, thinking she did not receive as many eggs as she ought to do from the girl who collected them,
asked a negro whether she ought to receive an egg from each hen a-day.
"It would be a very good hen to lay an egg every day," replied the negro.
Mistaking the meaning of the answer, and imagining that she had been
cheated, she gave the poor girl a flogging every time she failed to bring
the required number, notwithstanding all her protestations of innocence,
and frantic entreaties not to be whipped. At last a lady residing near, told
Mrs. R—— that it was absurd to expect anything of the kind. Colonel
R—— one day sent his servant-man to bring some groceries from the
stores; when he returned with the groceries, the Colonel said, "Why did
you bring me such inferior sugar as this?" The slave replied that it was
the same kind as he always had. The Colonel said it could not be so, as
the price was too low, adding, "go and tell Mr. V. at the stores to send me
some better at once." The slave went with the message; Mr. V. smiled,
and doubled the price on a new bill, and sent the same sugar back. The
Colonel looked first at the bill, and then at the sugar. "Aye, this is something like; this is as it ought to be," he said. I merely relate this anecdote
to show what kind of persons the slave-owners, in some instances, are,
and that the slaves are not always kept in subjection by a consciousness
of their master's intellectual superiority, for the slaves often, behind their
backs, laugh at their absurdities; but by a brutal system of terrorism practised upon them from their very birth.

   A circumstance of a different nature is the next I can call to mind.
The weather was warm and sultry, scarcely a breath of air stirred, and
clouds of an inky blackness began to rise from the distant uplands. Colonel R—— had just returned from his tobacco-fields; the rain began
to fall in large drops. "Bring in the niggers!" shouted Colonel R——.
Some fifteen or twenty soon entered his sitting-room, and were arranged
around the Colonel, who sat on a chair in the centre of the room. A distant thunder-clap was heard. "Come nearer," he cried, "stand close to

---

were Charles Randolph and Robert Randolph, both of whom owned plantations in Fauquier County.

me." And there sat this master of 500 niggers, cowering and trembling during the whole of the thunderstorm. I was told that this was his invariable custom whenever it thundered or lightened, imagining that the Almighty would not strike the slaves, consequently, being surrounded by them, the Colonel thought he should certainly escape. We slaves often talked together about this cowardice of Colonel R——'s, and attributed it to his fear of God, on account of his sins, although he was not a man remarkable for cruelty. But there is, even in the minds of those most accustomed to slavery, and born and brought up amongst it, a secret misgiving that all is not right; although, when no danger is near at hand, they will not only defend it, but eulogize it and expatiate upon its advantages, even to the negro himself. My mother told me that the Colonel thought the negroes could drive the lightning away. However, whether his conduct arose from this absurd notion or fear, it only proves the weak character of this tyrant over the souls and bodies of men.

My father and mother were slaves, and worked for different masters.[13] My mother had nine children, two boys and seven girls. The children are always the property of the mother's master.

Piety of Grandmother, a Native African.

My grandfather and grandmother were stolen from Africa and brought to Maryland, and taken from thence to Virginia. My grandmother was

13. In *Life and Sufferings* we are told, "My father was a slave, and worked for a tyrant master of the name of Carter; my mother was also a slave, and worked for a tyrant master of the name of Parker." Property tax lists for this area of Fauquier County in 1783 and 1778 include Alexander Parker and Richard Parker, both as owners of several slaves (mainly claimed to be under sixteen and therefore not subject to payment of tithes). A Charles Carter, one of several Carters in Virginia who owned a large number of slaves, is listed as owner of property on the eastern side of the Cedar Run. Alexander Parker's will and inventory (dated May and November 1785, respectively) list twenty slaves by name. The Fauquier County Courthouse records for 1816 show that Amy, the widow of Alexander Parker, and her two sons, William and Richard, had moved to Kentucky and were seeking to sell the land near the Cedar Run and bordering on the Walnut Branch, a smaller stream and area to the east of the Cedar Run and some twelve miles southeast of Warrenton.

taught by her young mistress to repeat the Prayers and Liturgy of the Protestant Church. My grandmother could not read, yet in spite of every disadvantage, she was very anxious about religion, and always eager to impart any religious knowledge she might have acquired to her children and grandchildren, or, in fact, to any one about her.

Systematic Degradation of Slave Children.

My grandmother showed she was actuated on every occasion by truly Christian principles. She wished very much to teach me the Prayers and Liturgy which she had learnt.

But the conduct of my master caused great perplexity to me, and made me indifferent about any such thing. My master was in the habit of sending for all the slave children from the cabins, then standing on the verandah, he would say, "Look! Do you see those horses?" "Yes, Sir," all replied together. "Do you see the cows?" "Yes, Sir." "Do you see the sheep?" "Yes, Sir." "Do you see the mules?" "Yes, Sir." "Look, you niggers! you have no souls, you are just like those cattle, when you die there is an end of you; there is nothing more for you to think about than living. White people only have souls." My mother, when I was a boy, had no notion of what religion is, and to my good grandmother alone I am indebted for any instruction I at this time received. She was ever, as I have said before, anxious to acquire religious knowledge and to attend prayer-meetings as often as she possibly could; for doing so on one occasion, I witnessed the first flogging I ever saw in my life. But before I describe the flogging, I will explain about the overseers. Many masters possessing large plantations, and some hundreds of slaves, being desirous to divest themselves as much as possible of the cares of managing the estate, hire white men, at a salary of from 1,200 to 1,400 dollars per annum, to look after the whole property. These are the best and most humane overseers. But other slave proprietors, in order to save the cost of an overseer, but chiefly to exact as much work as possible out of the niggers, make a nigger an overseer, who if he does not cruelly work the slaves is threatened with a flogging, which the master cannot give to a white man. In order to save his own back the slave overseer very often behaves in the most brutal manner to the niggers under him. My grandmother's master was one of the hard kind. He had made her son an overseer.

My Grandmother Flogged.

Consequently, my grandmother having committed the crime of attending a prayer-meeting, was ordered to be flogged by her own son. This was done by tying her hands before her with a rope, and then fastening the rope to a peach tree, and laying bare the back. Her own son was then made to give her forty lashes with a thong of a raw cow's-hide, her master standing over her the whole time blaspheming and threatening what he would do if her son did not lay it on.

My master had about 100 slaves, engaged chiefly in the cultivation of tobacco, this and wheat being the staple produce of Virginia at that time. The slaves had to work very hard in digging the ground with what is termed a grub hoe.[14] The slaves leave their huts quite early in the morning, and work until late at night, especially in the spring and fall. I have known them very often, when my master has been away drinking, work all night long, husking Indian corn to put into cribs.

Feeding of Slaves.

Slaves every Monday morning have a certain quantity of Indian corn handed out to them; this they grind with a handmill, and boil or use the meal as they like. The adult slaves have one salt herring allowed for breakfast, during the winter time. The breakfast hour is usually from ten to eleven o'clock. The dinner consists generally of black-eyed peas soup, as it is called. About a quart of peas is boiled in a large pan, and a small piece of meat, just to flavour the soup, is put into the pan. The next day it would be bean soup, and another day it would be Indian meal broth.

---

14. A heavy hoe with a large rectangular blade designed for uprooting plants, cutting tree roots, using in clay soil, and digging trenches.

The dinner hour is about two or three o'clock; the soup being served out to the men and women in bowls; but the children feed like pigs out of troughs, and being supplied sparingly, invariably fight and quarrel with one another over their meals. I remember when a boy I did not care how I was fed, all I was anxious about was to get sufficient. This mode of living is no doubt adopted for the express purpose of brutalizing the slaves as much as possible, and making the utmost difference between them and the white man. Slaves live in huts made of logs of wood covered with wood, the men and women sleeping indiscriminately together in the same room. But English people would be perfectly surprised to see the natural modesty and delicacy of the women thus huddled together; every possible effort being exerted, under such circumstances, to preserve appearances—an unchaste female slave being very rarely found.

As a lad, hearty, and only poorly fed, I was always delighted if I could get any extra food; and my memory seems to be very tenacious of anything having reference to eating. I remember my mother baking some short cake,[15] and giving a piece to me, and a piece to my cousin, who was a lad of my own age—eight or nine. I quickly dispatched mine; but my cousin danced about before me, with his piece, tantalizingly crying out, "I've got bread, and you've got none! I've got bread, and you've got none!" as rapidly as he could. I snatched the piece out of his hand, and ran away from him, and soon had a portion in my mouth. He threw himself down, and shouted, "I'm dead! I'm dead! I'm dead!" rolling, kicking, and screaming, as rapidly as he could, for full ten or fifteen minutes. His mother gave me a good beating that night. I felt very proud, however, and bragged about what I had done, for some days; but I made a great mistake soon after, which took me down a peg. I was wrestling with one of the children, and threw him, and hurt him, which displeased my grandmother, who said I should get a flogging. I made haste in the evening to get into the straw, and to cover myself with an old rug for the night. I began to snore away, as hard as I could, as if fast asleep; thinking they would not wake me to

15. Also called shortbread: a thick, sweet biscuit made with flour, sugar, butter or lard, and milk.

whip me. When my uncle came in, my grandmother said she had promised me a good flogging, and she would be as good as her word. My uncle
said, "Where is he? I'll give it to him." One of the women said, "There
he is, in his bed, asleep." I snored louder and faster. Another woman said,
"He is not asleep." "But he is asleep." "He isn't asleep." "But, me tell you,
he be asleep." Thus the women disputed. I thought I would help myself a
little, and said, "Yes, I be asleep!" I forgot. But my uncle did not forget to
take me out of the straw, and to flog me well.

My good grandmother's figure and general appearance will always be
indelibly impressed upon my mind. She was above the middle height in
England, and had short black hair, inclined to curl, but very sparse upon
the head. My grandfather was about six feet in height, a well-propor-
tioned, muscular man; his hair was longer than my grandmother's, and
very thick upon the head: from his appearance, I should suppose he was
not of the same tribe in Africa as my grandmother.

Grandmother's happy Death.

I never knew any woman so religious as my grandmother; in all her
oppressions and trials, her heart was full of the love of God. In looking
back now, after so many years, I am filled with admiration of her conduct. When any troubles had come to her, or when she had been whipped,
she would speak of her home, far away beyond the clouds, where there
would be no whipping, and she would be at rest. This seemed to be her
greatest, indeed her sole comfort, in the hour of trial. This would be a
source of joy, when seated, on a Sabbath evening, under the shade of the
peach trees, she talked to her fellow-slaves, or to those who came from
the neighbouring plantations to see her. I was standing by, one Sunday,
and heard a woman say to her, "Selling is worse than flogging. My husband was sold six years ago. My heart has bled ever since, and is not well
yet. I have been flogged many times, since he was torn from me, but my
back has healed in time."

My grandfather never was a professing Christian; his greatest stumbling-block was the conduct of the slaveholders, in buying and selling slaves, and then going, after doing so, and perhaps partaking of the Sacrament. "How," he would say, "can Jesus be just, if He will allow such oppression and wrong? Don't the slaveholders justify their conduct by the Bible itself, and say, that it tells them to do so? How can God be just, when He not only permits, but sanctions, such conduct?" My grandmother would reason with him, and endeavour to show him that the slaveholders, at the Last Day, would have to account for their actions, and that we slaves should look to our own conduct. However, no real, abiding change, such as had been produced upon my grandmother, ever was effected upon him.

As the closing scenes of life approached, my grandmother's faith became stronger and stronger. She looked forward to the future, when all would be set right; and delighted to talk about heaven, and to ask those about her to be good, that they might all meet together in the next world. Her illness was short; and ladies came to her bedside, for her good life was a subject of conversation even among them; and many a truthful lesson did they learn from her. She bore everything with Christian fortitude; her sons and daughters stood around her deathbed, receiving her blessing, or listening to her good advice. I was not present when she died, but my mother said she died gently and happily, as if her last hours were a foretaste of what was in store for her.

A badge of aristocracy among slaveholders is the number of slaves they hold, and white people of equal fortune are not generally allowed to visit slaveholders, who look down upon them with a species of contempt. One remarkable fact which I wish to impress upon my readers is this, that the white men born in those districts in America where slaves are held, are just as capable of bearing the heat as the black men. And the proof is this, that in the harvest-time, when the two are working together in the fields, the white men can actually beat the negroes at the work, and very often the black man has to give up, and is laughed at by the white labourer. They say, "Only give us sufficient wages, and we will work by the side of any nigger alive." It is quite shocking to hear slaveholders distorting even the Bible itself to prove that a negro alone was made for hard work.

Cunning of Slaves.

I remember a slave, who was not treated very well with respect to food and other things, when he had done his work being lectured by his mistress on the duties of a slave, she telling him that in proportion to his obedience and servility as a slave he would be loved by God. One day, on receiving the Bible from his mistress, he began as follows,—"Give your slaves plenty of bread and meat, and plenty of hot biscuit in a morning, also be sure and give him three horns of whiskey a-day." "Come, come, stop that, Bob," his mistress cried; "none of your nonsense, Bob, there is nothing of that kind there." Bob, throwing down the book, said, "There, there, take it yourself, read it; you says a great deal more than you'll find there." Slaves are all of them full of this sly, artful, indirect way of conveying what they dare not speak out, and their humour is very often the medium of hinting wholesome truths. Is not cunning always the natural consequence of tyranny? One of my master's neighbours had lost two pigs. The overseer was ordered to search the cottages to try to find any portions of the missing pigs. An old woman, who had one of the pigs, seeing the overseer coming to search, and having heard that the person who had stolen them was to receive 200 lashes when discovered, threw the pork, blood and all, into a tub of persimum, which is a kind of beer in America.[16] The overseer, having searched diligently all the nooks and corners of the cabin, even having opened the bed, said, "Well, Molly, I am very glad to find that you have not got the pigs. Now draw me some beer." Molly, with trembling hand, drew a bowl of it. "Why does your hand tremble, Molly?" said the overseer. "Because," said Molly, "old woman has been sick all night." "Very good, this beer," said the over-

---

16. In some states in the nineteenth century, a domestic beer was made from persimmons, a tawny golden fruit native to North America and described by early visitors as like a medlar.

seer; "draw me another." Molly now was frightened that the blood would betray her. She drew another bowl. "This is the very best beer I ever in my life tasted," said the overseer; "here is a shilling for you. I shall be sure and tell your master, Molly, that you have not got the pigs."

CHAPTER II.

*Scene on Leaving Virginia for Kentucky—Cross the Alleghany Mountains—
Arrive at my Master's New Plantation in Mason County—Become a House
Slave—Difficulties of Training me—A Burglar Encountered—Social
Affections of Slaves—A Sunday at Chapel—Christmas, how spent by the
Slaves—Slave Patrols—Brutalizing Effect of Slavery upon the Ladies—
Consequences to the Slaves of Resisting Tyranny.*

I had arrived at about my fourteenth year of age, without having been engaged in any definite employment,—running errands, tending the corn-fields, looking after the cattle, in short, doing anything and everything in turns about the plantation. My master had determined to give up his plantation in Virginia, and to go to another in Kentucky. I shall never forget the heart-rending scenes which I witnessed before we started. Men and women down on their knees begging to be purchased to go with their wives or husbands who worked for my master, children crying and imploring not to have their parents sent away from them; but all their beseeching and tears were of no avail. They were ruthlessly separated, most of them for ever. Still, after so many years, their wailings and lamentations and piercing cries sound in my ears whenever I think of Virginia.

Cross the Alleghany Mountains.[17]

We had to pass over the Alleghany mountains to Wieland, in New Virginia.[18] Wieland lies on the banks of the Ohio. We set out with sev-

17. The Allegheny Mountain Range (also spelled "Alleghany" and "Allegany") is part of the Appalachian Mountain Range. It runs from north to south for about 400 miles from central Pennsylvania through western Maryland, eastern West Virginia, and southwestern Virginia. The range is named after the Allegheny River. Its highest point is Spruce Knob, West Virginia (4, 863 feet).

18. "Wieland" seems to be a reference to Wheeling, in northern West Virginia.

eral waggons and a sorrowful cavalcade on our way to Kentucky. After several days' journey, we saw at a distance the lofty range of the Alleghany mountains. My master, by the use of his glass, had told us two or three days before that the mountains were near. They now became visible, looming in the distance something like blue sky. After a while we approached them, and began to pass over them through what appeared to be a long, winding valley. On every side, huge, blue-looking rocks seemed impending. I thought, if let loose, they would fall upon us and crush us. Our journey was, I may say, almost interrupted every now and then, by immense droves of pigs, which are bred in Kentucky, and were proceeding from thence to Baltimore, and other places in Virginia. These droves contained very often 700 or 800 pigs. When we halted for the night we lit our fires, and baked our Indian meal on griddles; sometimes the cakes were very much burnt, but these, together with salt herrings, were the only food we had. Our drink was water from the surrounding rills running down the mountain-sides. In fact, torrents of water, arising from the ice and melting snow, were rushing down in hundreds of directions. The scenery was what I may term hard and wild, the tops of the mountains being hid by the clouds, in many places rolling far beneath. But my thoughts in passing over these mountains then were rather those of amazement and wonder than those of a curious and inquiring mind, such as now, with some enlightenment, I might have. I only remember large flights of crows, and what are called in America, black birds, which make a loud screaming noise, instead of a beautiful note, like the English bird of this name.

Two or three times during the night, when we were encamped and fast asleep, one of the overseers would call our names over, every one being obliged to wake up and answer. My master was afraid of some of us escaping, so uncertain are the owners of the possession of their slaves. The masters are ever feverishly anxious about the slaves running away, and

---

Founded in 1769, Wheeling was a popular frontier town because of its position as a trade stop on the Ohio River. National Road, the nation's first roadway, reached Wheeling in 1818 from Cumberland, Maryland. In the nineteenth century, Wheeling became known as the "gateway to the West."

this being always continued, necessarily produces an irritability characteristic of the slave-holder. The howling of the wolves, and other wild animals, broke the solemn stillness which reigned widely around us. Now and then my master would fire his gun to frighten them away from us, but we never were in any way molested. Perhaps the fires kept them at a distance from us.

Arrive at my Master's new Plantation in Mason County.

From Welland[19] we took boats to Maysville, Kentucky. My master had bought a farm in Mason County, about twenty miles from Maysville.[20] When we arrived there we found a great deal of uncultivated land belonging to the farm. The first thing the negroes did was to clear the land of bush, and then to sow blue grass seed for the cattle to feed upon. They then fenced in the woods for what is called woodland pasture. The neighbouring planters came and showed my master how to manage his new estate. They told the slaves how to tap the sugar-tree to let the liquid out, and to boil it down so as to get the sugar from it. The slaves built a great many log-huts; for my master, at the next slave-market, intended to purchase more slaves.[21]

19. Another reference to Wheeling.

20. Mason County is in northeastern Kentucky and is in the heart of the fertile bluegrass area. Maysville became an important trading town on the banks of the Ohio River and opposite Ripley in the state of Ohio. In 1848 it replaced nearby Old Washington as the Mason county seat. It also became a significant point of departure for slaves escaping to the north. The county deeds show that William Parker acquired 134 acres on the North Fork in 1810 and another 1,500 acres in 1815. The North Fork is a tributary of the Licking River on the southwest border of Mason County. The will of Richard Parker, dated 1823, divides the 190 acres he owned by the waters of Stonelick Creek, which runs into the North Fork, to his sons, Alexander and Winslow. This area is near Orangeburg, approximately eight miles south of Maysville.

21. The 1860 census for Kentucky listed a total of 225,483 slaves, 10,684 free Negroes, and 919,484 whites. In 1833, Kentucky had introduced a nonimportation act, barring slaves from other states to be brought into Kentucky and sold at the markets. This act was repealed in 1849.

Become a House Slave.

I was taken into the house to learn to wait at table—a fortunate chance for me, since I had a better opportunity of getting food. I shall never forget my first day in the kitchen. I was delighted to see some bread in the pantry. I took piece after piece to skim the fat from the top of the boiling-pot, overjoyed that I could have sufficient.

Difficulties of Training me.

My mistress took a fancy to me, and began to teach me some English words and phrases, for I only knew how to say "dis" and "dat," "den" and "dere," and a few such monosyllables. It is a saying among the masters, the bigger fool the better nigger. Hence all knowledge, except what pertains to work, is systematically kept from the field-slaves. My mistress made me stand before her to learn from her how I was to take a message. "Now, Francis," she said, "I want to make you quite a ladies' man. You must always be very polite to the ladies. You must say, 'I will go and tell the ladies.'" I repeated some hundreds of times, "I will go and tell the ladies." After some days' training, she thought she had made me sufficiently perfect to deliver a message. "Francis!" "Yes, marm," I said. "Go and tell Mrs. ——— that I shall feel obliged by her calling upon me at half-past twelve o'clock to-morrow." "Yes, marm," I said; and she made me repeat the message some dozens of times. When perfect, as she thought, away I went, repeating all the way, "Missis will feel obliged by your calling upon her at half-past twelve; Missis will," &c., until I met a gentleman on the road who had seen and heard me repeating the words over and over again before I saw him. He called out, "Whom are you talking to?" I jumped, and every word jumped out of me, for I forgot it all. I ran back to my mistress and told her I had forgotten it, but did not tell her the reason why. "Just as I thought," she said. The teaching re-commenced, and, after some scores of repetitions of the message, I started again, determined that no one should hear me. I went whispering the words all the way as fast as ever I could, hastened into the lady's house, and hurriedly said the words over two or three times to the lady, and then ran back. Upon one occasion my mistress's sister said that she wanted me to do some washing, and gave me a dress to wash. I picked it up, and put it on the wash-board, and immediately tore it on purpose. She had left the room to fetch some thing for me to wash it with, and, returning in a minute, "Francis," she said, "I hope you have not begun to wash that dress yet?" "Oh, yes, missis, I have," I answered, holding up the torn dress at the same time. "You blockhead!" she said, "I shall never be able to teach you anything; I can never drive anything into your thick skull. I have a good mind to take a stick and kill you, you worthless good-for-nothing." But I was sufficiently cunning by this stratagem to escape what appeared to me the degrading womanly occupation of washing. In the same way I acted when she attempted to teach me to milk the cow. By no possible ingenuity could she, as she thought, make me learn the right side of the cow to milk upon; consequently, the cow invariably kicked when I was on the wrong side, and upset the milk-pail. I saw one day some cotton drying by the fire; I thought I would try whether I could make it blaze, thinking, if it did, I could easily put it out. I lit a stick, and set the cotton on fire. Every one in and about the house rushed to the kitchen to extinguish the flame; after some time they succeeded. I told my mistress that a spark had fallen upon it and made it blaze. This story seemed to satisfy her at the time. Some weeks afterwards my mistress called me into her room, and gave me some treacle and bread, and asked me if it was sweet. "Yers, missis," I said. "We are very good friends now, are we not?" "Yers, missis." She gave me two more pieces. "Now, Francis," she said, "don't friends always tell one another the truth?" "Yers, missis." "Don't friends tell each other every thought?" "Yers, missis." "Now, Francis," she added, fixing her eyes fully upon mine, "did you not set fire to the cotton?" "Ye-ye-yers, missis," I replied. "Now you shall have a good whipping for your lies and for setting fire to the cotton," she said; and sure enough I was flogged right soundly.

My mistress's sister was writing a letter one morning; I looked over her shoulder, and thought what pretty marks she was making. Having half finished one line, she put her pen down and left the room to take her breakfast. I took the pen up, and completed the line with crooks, and commenced another line, and ended just under the part where she had left off. I was examining what I had done, thinking it looked better and more distinct than hers, when in darted my mistress's sister, and began to beat me most unmercifully. "What has he done? what has he done?" cried my uncle, who was cook, and utterly at a loss to know what I had been doing. "The young rascal has been spoiling my writing," she said, laying on all the time, until my back was severely cut. I thought at the time it was cruel. A day or two afterwards my mistress took me into her room and talked to me kindly; she said it was wicked to do such things as those for which I had been flogged. I was surprised at a good deal of what she said, for I did not understand exactly in what the wrong consisted.

I merely mention these three or four little incidents to show how grossly ignorant I was, and that what is known to a child mixing in civilized society is a complete mystery and puzzle even to men working in the fields in a state of slavery. It was found utterly impossible to get on with me in the house unless I was instructed in something. But the most debasing ignorance is systematically kept up amongst the outdoor hands, any one manifesting superior intelligence being weeded out of the working gang, lest he should spoil the other slaves. My mistress was anxious to teach me to pick some wool. "You must pick it very quickly," she said. "Your master's brother will watch you, and tell me if you don't." She placed me in a room where my master's brother's portrait hung on the wall. "There he is," she said, "looking at you. Now, mind, you must pick away as fast as you can. Don't stop, or he will come and tell me." I thought it was my master's brother, and worked as hard as I could until I became very thirsty. I stopped, and looked anxiously at him, went up to him, and, putting my hand to my head, "Please, massa," I said, "may I go and get a drink?" He did not answer. This occurred for several days, until at last I thought I never saw a man who did not wink. I went slowly and cautiously up to the picture, and, after some hesitation, I felt it and turned it over, looked at the back, and, whilst thus engaged, in came my mistress. "What are you doing there," she said, "I will teach you to mind your work"; and she took the horsewhip and gave me a good flogging. She was no doubt annoyed that I had found out she was fooling me. When working within sight of the picture afterwards, I would say, "I's not going to work. You don't know nothing. They don't give us nothing. I's not going to work for nothing." And I did not half work, only just doing a little.[22]

A remarkable incident occurred soon after I was in our new house, and it evidently had a great deal to do with making me a favourite amongst them.

A Burglar Encountered.

I was sleeping one night, when my master was from home, on a mat near the foot of my mistress's bed. She called out to me, "Francis, Francis! get up! get up! come here! look!" pointing out of the window, "there is some one trying to break into the house." I saw a man climbing up a ladder, which he had placed against the wall. "Missis, oh, missis!" I said, "I'll put de poker in de fire," and in an instant I thrust the poker into the fire. We stood watching the movements of the man, my mistress trembling and being very frightened. He ascended the ladder, and cautiously opened the window, and put his arm in as if feeling. I seized the poker out of the fire and thrust it up his sleeve. "Oh, Lord!" he cried out, and instantly threw himself down from the top of the ladder and disappeared, no doubt well burnt.

My mistress was delighted with my quickness in devising in a moment such a scheme, and always took great pleasure in relating the adventure to any visitors, so that I was looked upon as a faithful and intelligent lad.

Another incident tended also to attach my mistress to me. My grandfa-

22. The trope of the portrait that is said to watch over a slave in the master's absence also occurs in *The Interesting Narrative of the Life of Olaudah Equiano, or Gustavus Vassa, the African, Written by Himself,* ed. Vincent Carretta (Harmondsworth, U.K.: Penguin, 1995), 63. This series of anecdotes, like several later ones, seems at first glance to have two rather contradictory purposes: on the one hand, they reveal Francis's relative ignorance regarding the speech and culture of his owners, and his eagerness to acquire them; on the other, they demonstrate his cunning and intelligence when he seeks to subvert their authority and cultural assumptions regarding the inherent "stupidity" of slaves by pretending to endorse them.

ther had gone to the mill for some meal. He got drunk, the bag of meal fell from the horse's back, and the pigs devoured the meal whilst my grandfather had gone for some one to help him. When he returned home, my master said, "Will, where is the meal?" My grandfather said, "Don't ask me about the meal; the pigs have eaten it up." My master said, "I will give you a beating." "You had better try it on," said my grandfather. They both began to wrestle with one another. My master tried to get hold of the hair of my grandfather, but, being nearly bald, this was impossible; but my grandfather pulled the hair out of my master's head by handfuls. I danced about in great distraction to see them contending with one another, and ran and got a bowl of water, and threw it on them both, which instantly made them gasp and desist from the struggling. My master fetched the horsewhip, and threatened to kill me for throwing the water, but, at the intercession of my mistress, I escaped. My mistress, the next day, said, "Francis, what made you throw that water on your master and your grandfather?" I said, "Missis, don't you know?" She said, "No." I said, "When ladies and gemmens come to see you and the dogs come wid 'em, dey come in de kitchen, and our dogs jump at 'em, dey get to fighting, den my uncle he throw de cold water on dem, and dat part 'em. Missis, I thought you always know'd dat we parted de dogs in dat way."

Social Affections of Slaves.

I went about this time to see several person baptized, all adults, both black and white, and I shall never forget the anxiety displayed by the black men when their wives were being dipped. The black men protested that their wives were held under the water longer than the white women, although there was not a shade of difference in the time of the immersion. The affection of the men for their wives and children would be noticed by any one. The men never, if possible, allow their wives to carry the young ones, but are always delighted to have them in their arms, and to walk by the side of the women. (A slave possessing nothing, and rarely hoping to possess anything, except a wife and children, has all his affections concentrated upon them; hence often, when torn from them, he pines away and dies.) The social affections are so strong, that no hard usage can weaken them. Indeed, brutality, on the part of the master, seems to make the slave cling closer and closer; thus intensifying his sufferings, when the "trader" comes to tear him away.[23]

In answer to a question, which has often been put to me, I may here state, that no slave-children are ever christened: a name is agreed upon between the black woman and her mistress, or her mistress's daughters. They take a Bible in their hands, and say, let such be the name.

When I was about fourteen years of age, my mother whipped me, because I had hurt one of my sisters in play. I felt very ill after it, and thought if I feigned to be dead, she would get a whipping. I began to groan out. The women in the spinning-room ran out, thinking I was dying. My mistress's sister, and two young lady visitors, ran into the room; and, feeling I was cold, and noticing that I breathed but slowly—which I was managing, as well as I could, taking a good gasp every time—they turned me over. They also were afraid that I was dying. They began to cry, which brought my mistress into the kitchen. She began to cry, at first; and then, looking steadfastly at me, "Stand by," she said, taking out a pin, unseen by me, she thrust it right into me. I struck out with my feet, and sent a black woman, who had been rubbing me, sprawling on the ground. I hollered out, "Oh! oh! oh!" until they could hear me a mile off. Some ran away instantly, from fear; others burst into loud fits of laughter; my mistress joining in the laugh. "Well," she said, "I never saw such an artful nigger in all my life. He is always up to some of his tricks."

I had a tolerably good time of it now, being in the kitchen, helping to cook, or waiting at the table, listening eagerly to any conversation going on; and thus learning many things of which the field-hands were totally ignorant.

23. Fedric and/or his scribe here emphasize the close affection between black men and their wives and children in response to claims by slave owners and their supporters that such affections were trifling or nonexistent among black people. Fedric also seeks here and in other passages to appeal to the increasing importance given to family units and domesticity in nineteenth-century England and North America, as seen also in Harriet Beecher Stowe's *Uncle Tom's Cabin*.

A Sunday at Chapel.

On Sundays we were sent to chapel; all the slaves being seated in the galleries, apart from the white people.

Mr. Pain,[24] the minister, was absent from chapel one Sabbath; but, appearing next Sunday, he explained his absence by informing his congregation that two of his slaves had run away. Immediately, there was a general lamentation, because brother Pain had lost his slaves, and many calculations were made about their value. The following Sunday, the minister, with a face radiant with joy, announced to his audience that his slaves had been brought back to him. On hearing this, a hubbub of delight pervaded the chapel; but when he further informed them that he had administered to each eighty lashes, in order to teach them their duty, and to deter them and others from running away in future, the audience were overjoyed; one saying to another, "Brother Pain has done perfectly right. He has taught them, and all the slaves who hear, what their duty is, and how they are to be dealt with, if they attempt to run away."

When first I came to England, I was surprised to find every clergyman and Dissenting minister,[25] to a man, denouncing slavery as contrary to Christianity. But the reverse is the case in the Southern States of America. All the Methodists, Baptists, and Independents—in fact, every minister of religion—uphold slavery, and defend it by passages from the very same Book out of which the clergy, in this country, make quotations to condemn it.

I leave the natural inference to be drawn by themselves; merely sug-

---

24. Probably William Payne, who is listed in the U.S. census for 1810 as a "Minister of the Gospel" living in Mason County. According to the census records, he had at that time eighteen slaves. The Methodist Episcopal Church in Old Washington, which was then the Mason county seat, was built with a separate slave gallery (removed during renovation in the 1970s).

25. The term *Dissenter* refers to several Protestant denominations—including Presbyterians, Baptists, Quakers, and Congregationalists—that eschewed the Anglican communion and rejected other doctrines maintained by the Church of England. Until 1828, such preachers refusing to take an oath of allegiance to the Church of England were, like Roman Catholics, excluded from civil or military office in England or Wales.

gesting, that, perhaps, self-interest may, in other cases also, cause fatal delusions and compliances.

Christmas, how spent by Slaves.

About Christmas, my master would give four or five days' holiday to his slaves; during which time he supplied them plentifully with new whiskey, which kept them in a continual state of the most beastly intoxication. He often absolutely forced them to drink more, when they had told him they had had enough. He would then call them together, and say, "Now, you slaves, don't you see what bad use you have been making of your liberty? Don't you think you had better have a master, to look after you, and make you work, and keep you from such a brutal state, which is a disgrace to you, and would ultimately be an injury to the community at large?" Some of the slaves, in that whining, cringing manner, which is one of the baneful effects of slavery, would reply, "Yees, Massa; if we go on in dis way, no good at all."

Thus, by an artfully-contrived plan, the slaves themselves are made to put the seal upon their own servitude. The masters, by the system, are rendered as cunning and scheming as the slaves themselves.[26]

"Joe," said a master, "if you will work well for me, you shall be buried in my grave." The slave said nothing in reply, but thought, Massa is a bad man, and that he would not like to be buried near him. The slave thought he had been too near his master all his life, and had rather be away from him, when he died. Seeing the slave idling, "Joe," shouted his master, "have you forgotten what I promised you, if you work well?" "No, Massa, me remember; but me don't want." "What for, Joe?" "Be-

---

26. Compare Frederick Douglass regarding the encouragement for slaves to drink heavily over the Christmas holidays, a practice Douglass declares to be "among the most effective means in the hands of the slaveholder in keeping down the spirit of insurrection. . . . These holidays serve as conductors, or safety valves, to carry off the rebellious spirit of enslaved humanity." *Narrative of the Life of Frederick Douglass, an American Slave: Written by Himself*, ed. Houston A. Baker, Jr. (Harmondsworth, UK: Penguin, 1982), 115.

cause de debbil might some day come, and steal me away, in mistake for you, Massa." His master was silent on this subject ever afterwards.

Slave Patrols.

On New Year's Day ten white men are chosen, who are called patrols; they are sworn-in at the court-house, and their special duty is to go to the negro cabins for the purpose of searching them to see whether any slaves are there without a pass or permit from their masters. The head of the ten is called Captain. He sends the men into the cabins, waiting outside himself at some distance with the horses, the patrol being a mounted body. If any slaves are found without a pass they are brought out, and being made to strip are flogged, the men receiving ten and the women five lashes each.

Brutalizing Effect of Slavery upon the Ladies.

This is looked upon as great fun by the patrol and the white people, young ladies and gentlemen from the verandahs laughing and enjoying the scene.

When I have told of my being flogged, I often hear persons in this country say, "Oh! but he should not have whipped me in that manner; I would have resisted, I would have done this, that, or the other." But, my dear reader, I will tell you a true story, what I know and saw.

Consequences to the Slaves of Resisting Tyranny.

Two slaves, who were perhaps not so completely cowed as the rest, said to my master, who was about to flog them, "No, massa, we not going to be flogged so much, we won't submit." "What is that you say?" my master said, starting back. They repeated, "We are not going to allow you to beat us as you have done." "How will you prevent it?" he said. "You'll see, you'll see, massa," speaking half threateningly. He was evidently afraid of them. When they went home at night he spoke mildly to them, and told them he only wanted them to do their work, that it would be better if they could get on in the fields without him. "Don't hurry yourselves, my boys." For two or three days he never went much among them, and when he did he spoke in a very quiet, subdued manner. But mounted negroes were sent with letters to all the plantations around. The slaves had been sent to a species of barn where they shell the Indian corn. Suddenly above a hundred slaveholders, armed with revolvers, marched from different points, and at one time, evidently agreed upon, surrounded the place where the negroes were. All the slaves were ordered out, and the two who had refused to be flogged were made to strip, and my master first had one tied up, and flogged him as hard as he could for some time, the poor slave calling out, "Oh, pray, massa! Oh, pray, massa!" My master, pausing to take breath, one of the slaveholders said, "I would not flog him in that way, I would put him on a blacksmith's fire, and have the slaves to hold him until I blew the bellows to roast him alive." Then my master started again and flogged until the poor fellow was one mass of blood and raw flesh. The other was tied up and served in a similar manner, one of the slaveholders saying he ought to be tied to a tree and burnt alive. And now I would ask, How can an unarmed, an unorganized, degraded, cowed set of negroes prevent this treatment? The slaveholders can and do flog them to death, and nothing more is thought of it than of a dog being killed, and not so much.[27]

27. The *Maysville Eagle* reported on July 11, 1837, that the slave owners of Mason County had organized themselves into a society "for the purpose of concerted measures for the better security of our slave property."

CHAPTER III.

Negroes' Wedding—Vanity Exposed—Love of Long Words—Death
of my old Master—Cruelly treated by my dissipated young Master—
Slaves sold to pay my Master's Gambling Debts—Slaveholder's
own Children sold to Infamy.

The first wedding which I remember being at certainly afforded a good deal of amusement to me and others who were present. I will, therefore, endeavour to describe it as well as I can. The black man was named Jerry, and his intended, Fanny.[28] Jerry went to learn from Fanny's master and mistress whether they would allow him to take her for his wife. Fanny's mistress said, "Jerry, do you love her?" He said, "Yers, marm." "How do you know?" she said. "Because me lub ebery ting on de plantation since me lub Fanny,—de hosses, and all de tings on de plantation seems better dan anybody else's. It seems to me Fanny got de best missis in de country; me give most anyting if me could fall into dis family," said Jerry. Mr. Ord,[29] Fanny's master, said, "Come, Elizabeth, you must let him have

28. The inventory taken in 1826 following Richard Parker's death includes two slaves named Jerry and Fanny (Mason County Courthouse Records, Will Book G, 169). However, both these names are commonly found among slaves listed at this time and in Mason County—e.g., George Morton's 1837 will bequeaths several slaves, including Nancy, Fanny, and Mary, to his children and grandchildren; and his inventory (1841, Mason County Courthouse Records, Will Book M, 256) includes Jerry among twenty-one slaves.

29. Ord is perhaps a mishearing of "Hord." Several branches of the Hord family emigrated from Virginia to Mason County in the late eighteenth century, and appear as slave owners in the 1850 and 1860 slave schedules for Mason County. The name of Francis Hord appears frequently as a signatory on the wills and deeds relating to the Parker families. Francis Triplett Hord (1797–1869), of Beechland, near Maysville, is listed as the owner of nineteen slaves. In early manhood he was a surveyor, studied law, was admit-

her." She said, "Well, Jerry, you can have her, but we don't whip Fanny, and you must not whip her." Jerry bowing low, said, "No, missis, if she never get a whipping till me gives it to her, she'll neber get one, cause me lub her too well to whip her." Fanny's mistress said, "Because I know if you were to whip her, she would not deserve it, and I should never let you come on the premises again." Jerry replied, "By de time me have had her one year me know you'll give me as good name as Fanny, for Fanny's mistress shall be my mistress, and Fanny's master shall be my master." "Well, Jerry," said Fanny's mistress, "you must bring January's Tom[30] or Morton's Gilbert[31] to marry you, two weeks from this night, if your master and mistress consent, and tell your master and mistress that we have agreed to give Fanny a supper, and we shall be very glad to see them, since we are going to have a great many ladies and gentlemen come to see the wedding." Jerry in ecstasy answered, "Yers, marm; thank you thousand and thousand times, missis."

On the Saturday night appointed, Jerry went with January's Tom to Fanny's master's. Jerry had a pair of black trousers of his master's on, a little too large in the leg, and a coat fitting very well, except that the tails were too long; some one had given him a white waistcoat and a white cravat, which was only a little less stiff than its wearer, and a pair of white gloves, contrasting very much with the coal black of Jerry's shining face. Fanny's mistress had dressed her in a white muslin gown and very nice light shoes, her head being decked with white and red artificials,[32] made from goose's down, which accorded well with her woolly hair. Her bridesmaid was attired somewhat similarly, only with not quite so many artificials. The happy pair were seated in the middle of a large kitchen;

ted to the bar, and became one of the leaders of the Kentucky bar, ranking with the first men of his state. He held the office of circuit judge.

30. Samuel January, who lived in Walnut Street, Limestone (now Maysville), owned several slaves. However, his will dated 1837 mentions only "Betty and her increase."

31. The inventory for George Morton, of Maysville, following his death in 1841 lists twenty slaves, including Tom and Cuthbert (but not Gilbert). It is possible that "Gilbert" is either a misremembering by Fedric or mishearing by the transcriber of "Cuthbert."

32. Artificial flowers or leaves made from fabric and feathers.

Fanny had a very pleasant countenance, a tawny complexion, and was admired very much by her mistress and her friends, but most of all by Jerry. He was asked if he would have her. "Yers, indeed me will," he said. Fanny was very bashful, and spoke very low, and bowed. "Come, where is the parson?" said her mistress, "it is time for him to be marrying them." "Parson!" some of the ladies called out, "Parson!" At the sound of this dignified title, bolt upright jumped January's Tom. "Marm, yers, marm." "It is time for you to marry them." "Yers, marm, yers, marm!" said Tom.

Now, January's Tom not being able to read, had listened to his master's grandson reciting the marriage service until he had it by heart, and as luck or mischief would have it, the Prayer-book was laid upside down. Tom now commenced, with the book in this position, to read the service, amidst the infinite mirth of the ladies, who every now and then glanced over his shoulder at the inverted book. Tom, however, thinking all the laughter was at the happy couple, persevered in the most solemn manner. Having finished repeating the marriage service to the satisfaction of all, Fanny's mistress said, "Parson, make him salute his wife." Now, Jerry being a field hand, knew nothing about this grammar word "salute."[33] "What! do what?" he said. "Salute your bride," said the parson. "Wh-a-t! do what?" said Jerry, as much puzzled as if it had been a Chinese word. Perceiving the perplexity, Fanny's mistress said, "Parson, tell him to kiss his wife." The parson said, "Kiss your wife." Jerry said, "Do you mean me to 'bus' her? What for you not tell me afore?" and instantly seizing Fanny round the neck, he made the room resound with the smacks, amidst the roars of laughter of all, until Fanny's mistress told him that would do, when, reluctantly, he desisted.

Fanny's master then wished Jerry to tell the company how he got his wife. He said, "Ladies and gemmen, me will tell you how me come to see Fanny. Me went to see Mr. Marshall's Charlotte for two years, she promised to hab me. Me promised to bring her a straw bonnet, but de grubs

---

33. "Grammar" here is used not simply to refer to correct syntax but to suggest sophisticated and educated use of language.

had eaten all on my truck-patch (the piece of ground allotted by some good masters for the slave to cultivate for his own benefit). Me went to see Charlotte on de Sunday, and she asked me to sit down in de kitchen, and she say, 'Where de bonnet?' Me told her de reason me didn't get it. And she said, 'You worthless nigger, you can't hab me,' and she run de fork into my arm, and me run home and say, 'De debble must be in dat gal.' Me went, to see good many gals after dat; me see good many like Charlotte, but me wouldn't stop, me leave, till me come to see Fanny. She seem to be good natured gal, but she hab me come to see her good while afore she say she hab me. Me tell her dat me lub her better dan all de people in de world. She say, 'if she could believe dat, she would hab me.' Me said me would treat her kind, and treat our chilun kind; but when me say dis about de chilun, she ran out of de house, and me didn't see her of three or four weeks apter dat. Me den see her, but me didn't tink dat she would run de fork in my arm, as Charlotte did. Fanny ask me 'if me rebberence her.' Me say, 'Fanny, don't know what you mean.' She say, 'Massa rebberence Missis, and you must rebberence me.' Me say, 'Oh, yes, to be sure; and you be good to me?' She say, 'If you be kind to me, I be kind to you.' And dat made me feel happy."

Thus ended Jerry's interesting account of his courtship.

Then about 300 slaves, friends of the happy couple, sat down to a good supper. Fanny being a house-servant, presided, with considerable tact, at the head of the table, and Jerry at the opposite end, in rather a confused and awkward, but good-humoured manner. A bottle of whiskey was on the table, and Jerry was called upon to give a toast. "Me don't know what you mean by de toast," said Jerry. Fanny's mistress said, "We'll tell you." He said, "Me can't talk, but me do as well as me can. Dis is my heart dat will be talking to you. Me hope Fanny's massa and missis neber will come to want, and me hope all de family, when dey die, may go to heben, and me hope dat Fanny and myself neber will be parted from each other, nor our chilun." At the last word all laughed heartily.

During twenty years after their wedding, I knew this happy pair, with a dutiful family of sons and daughters around them. A kind Providence had granted poor Jerry's prayer; a good master and an indulgent mistress were vouchsafed to them, on the same plantation their children were, some of them working, and the little ones playing about; and my sincere wish is, that no change of their master's fortune may send the "dealer" to tear asunder those whom affection of the purest kind had so firmly cemented together.

Vanity Exposed.

Having been made cook, I got on for some time tolerably well, sending up the dinners in first-rate style, exerting myself to the utmost, for I had a favour to ask, and I knew the best way to get at the hearts of my master and mistress was through their stomachs. I had noticed three or four watches hanging about the house, and one very old-fashioned, and evidently not of much value; I thought I should like to have it to wear on a Sunday at chapel. I asked my mistress, who was friendly towards me, to intercede with my master for the loan of it. "Yes, Francis," she said; "be a good fellow; manage the dinners well." "Yers, missis," I said, "I am sure to do that." And, sure enough, all was dished up carefully. In the course of a short time the watch was given to me, and off I went to the chapel, having made myself as spruce as possible. On my way, every time I passed any one I pulled my watch out to display it. I walked up into the gallery of the chapel and looked down upon my fellow negroes without watches as ten degrees beneath me in point of dignity. During the sermon I pulled out the watch several times, catching the eye of the preacher. At last he paused, and, looking at me, he said, "Ah! that must be a very good negro, a very good negro indeed; I see he has got a watch. Pray ," looking steadfastly at me, "can you tell me what o'clock it is?" I looked hastily at my watch, and replied, "Five o'clock." Instantly there was a loud laugh through the chapel, for it was only half-past twelve. My mistress ridiculed me afterwards, and said she could teach me nothing, and all my fellow negroes made me a perpetual butt for their jokes. The fact was, I knew no more about the watch than the watch knew about me.

Love of Long Words.

I one day overheard a young lady who was visiting at our house say to my mistress, "My intended will be here in a few days, I wish you would have everything put right." I thought, "When he comes, I'll hear what he has to say to you, and then I shall know how to court the black girls when I go out." Two or three days afterwards the young gentleman arrived, and I was on the alert to hear what he had to say to the young lady. I thought I heard him say, "Miss, I do admire your beauty, I respect your ingenuity, and I adore your virtue; I do love you, because I cannot help it." I was listening like a cat watching for a mouse. I repeated what I had heard over and over again until I got it perfect, and I then felt proud, because I thought I should have something superior to say when I went among the girls. But the next time I listened I made a great mistake. I heard a gentleman who was talking to some young ladies say, "I learnt my grammar well when I went to school." In a few minutes afterwards I heard him make use of the word characteristic. I thought he said, "cutting up sticks." I was delighted, and went on repeating "cutting up sticks." I thought it was a nice grammar word to speak when I should go among the black girls. The first time when I went among some who were having a little spree, a black man was seated by a very nice girl I knew; I said to her, "I can speak grammar." She said, "You can? what is it?" I said, "It is cutting up sticks." She gave the black man a blow with her elbow and said, "Go away; I am going over to sit with our friend; he can speak grammar; it's cutting up sticks." It was sometime before I found out my mistake. I knew I could not learn anything from the slaves, and I was, therefore, constantly listening to the gentlemen and ladies, and endeavouring to learn as many words as possible from them. Many times I was mistaken, but, right or wrong, I could march into a room with fullblown importance, and cut out a dozen men by bumptiously repeating anything which I had overheard. The black girls always like something which is a little better than common conversation.

The Death of my old Master.

I was about twenty-eight or thirty years of age when my old master was seized with a fever. He was upwards of seventy years of age, and, prior to this, had been a healthy man.[34] No change whatever of a serious nature had taken place in his conduct or conversation; indeed, a few days before the fever, he had been cursing and blaspheming at a slave-woman. When he was taken ill, the family wished to send for a doctor. "No," he said, "I know it is of no use; I shall die." However, one was sent for. Some of the planters, his neighbours, came, to be with him, and, as the fever increased, he began to rave and cry out, "Oh, take it away! take it away!" One of the slaveholders was very much frightened, for he also thought that he saw something. In a few days my master died, but he never made any sign that he had any hope for the future. His will had been recently made, his slaves were apportioned to his four children, and his son said that his father had never wished them to free the slaves.[35]

Cruelly treated by my dissipated young Master.

My young master now was about twenty-four or twenty-five years of age; he did not seem to mourn much for his lost father, but said, "You slaves have been living upon white bread, but I will soon teach you something different from that. You shall now have the treatment proper for niggers. I have been wishing for some time to tan your hides for you." Of course his discourse was interlarded with oaths and curses, with which I

34. Census records for Mason County (Eastern District) for 1820 and 1830 suggest that Richard Parker, listed as aged between fifty and sixty in the 1830 census, may be the master referred to here. According to the 1830 census, he owned eight slaves, including a male between twenty-four and thirty-six years old, who may have been Francis.

35. A will for Richard Parker was recorded in 1847, leaving all his slaves and property to his son, Addison S. Parker (Mason County Courthouse Records, Willbook O, 11–13). At this date, Francis would have been forty-one or forty-two, according to his own estimate of the year of his birth, not twenty-eight or thirty. Later in the narrative, Francis mentions that it is now (at the time of dictation) fourteen years since his first attempted escape and severe whipping, which would place that episode in 1848 or 1849.

cannot pollute my page. I soon began to wish that I was a field-hand, for day by day he was drunk and hanging about the kitchen.

I began to have a terrible life of it. A few years before his father's death, he had led a riotous, dissipated life, losing money by gambling, and then borrowing. All his neighbours were astonished at the amount of his debts, for the sheriff's officers were constantly on the premises. No doubt the state of his circumstances made him drink more.

Slaves Sold to pay my Master's Gambling Debts.

The slaves are in general the first property parted with, a dozen likely niggers bringing in a tolerably round sum. Aunt Aggy was the first slave sold; she had a little boy eight or nine years of age, and when she was driven to the chained gang on the road he ran after her, crying, "Mother—mother; oh my mother." My master ordered one of the slaves to fetch him the wagon whip. He took it and lashed the poor little fellow round the neck and legs until he fell down, then he flogged him until he got up again, and still my master cut at him until the boy shrieked out dreadfully, writhing in agony, the blood streaming down his little legs. His mother was driven off with the gang, and her little boy never saw her more. In three or four weeks after this, a "trader" was seen talking to my master. The slaves were in a state of consternation, saying, "Is it me? Is it me? Who'll go next?" One of the slaves said, "See, they are selling the pigs to go to Virginia. They don't seem to care, but we can't be like pigs, we can't help thinking about our wives and children."

The slaves were all taking their dinners in their cabins about two o'clock. My master, the "trader," and three other white men walked up to the cabins, and entered one of them. My master pointed first to one, and then to another, and three were immediately handcuffed, and made to stand out in the yard. One of the slaves sold had a wife and five children on another plantation; another slave had a wife and three children; and the other had a wife and one child. My master, the dealer, and the others then went into another large cabin, where there were eight or nine women feeding the children with Indian-meal-broth. My master said,

"Take your pick of the women." The poor things were ready to drop down. The "trader" said, "I'll give you 800 dollars for that one." My master said, "I'll take it." The "trader," touching her with a long cane he had in his hand, said, "Walk yourself out here, and stand with those men." She jumped up and laid her child out of her arms in an old board-cradle, and walked to the chained men. My master said, "Take your pick of the rest." The "trader" looked round and said, "I'll give you 750 dollars for that one." "I'll not take it," my master replied. "What will you take?" said the "trader"; "what is the least you'll take?" My master answered, "Not a dollar less than I took for the other." The "trader" paused a minute or two, surveying her, and then said, "I'll give it." Then, holding his cane out, said, sternly, "Walk out of this, and stand with those men." She laid her child in one of the women's arms, and speaking low, said, "Take care of my child, if you please." The women were so terrified that they dared not say a word, for three or four weeks before this time this very "trader" had given 1,000 dollars for a slave to a Mr. W., a neighbouring planter. The slave had said it was hard for him to be carried away from his wife and children, the "trader" instantly beat him so unmercifully, that Mr. W. thought the poor slave would be killed, and said, "You are not going to throw away your money in that way, are you?" "I don't care," said the "trader," "I have bought him, he is mine, and for one cent. I would kill him. I never allow a slave to talk back to me after I have bought him." He had beaten the poor fellow so severely that he could not walk. The "trader" said to Mr. W. he should be passing that way again in about a month, and if they would take care of the slave and cure him, he would pay the damage, and either call or send for him.

The three men and two women were driven out to the gang on the highway, and chained together, two and two. We never heard of them again. One of the wives left behind was nearly driven mad, she took it so to heart. No doubt those sent away were quickly used up in the sugar plantations and rice swamps of the South. But the masters soon replace the dead ones with others. There is an abundant supply in the markets of the breeding States, of all kinds, field and house hands, some bringing long prices, so that a slave owner finds the sale of them the readiest mode of extricating himself from any pecuniary difficulty.

Slaveholders' own Children Sold to Infamy.

Even his own child, by a black woman or a mulatto, when the child is called a quadroon, and is very often as white as any English child, is frequently sold to degradation. I knew a ———— S——, Esq.; he sold his own daughter, a quadroon, to a gentleman of New Orleans for 1,500 dollars, who said "he only wanted her to be housekeeper for him, and to be mistress over the other niggers, and to do just as he wanted her, for he had no wife." This startled the poor girl, who said she would not have cared if she had been going to marry him. She took it very much to heart, and so did her unhappy mother, especially when she heard her child say, "Oh, mother, I hope there will come a day when those left behind will not be forced as I shall be." And surely that day is being heralded in now, amidst the flaming homesteads and the slaughter of the sons and dishonour of the daughters of these heartless oppressors of their fellow-man, aye, of their own flesh and blood. There are thousands upon thousands of mulattoes and quadroons, all children of slaveholders, in a state of slavery. Slavery is bad enough for the black, but it is worse, if worse can be, for the mulatto or the quadroon to be subjected to the utmost degradation and hardship, and to know that it is their own fathers who are treating them as brutes, especially when they contrast their usage with the pampered luxury in which they see his lawful children revel, who are not whiter, and very often not so good-looking as the quadroon.

I remember, one bright moonlight night, a fine young man, a quadroon, stripping his shirt off, and showing me his lacerated back. He cried, and I cried too, to see him in such a state. He said the next time his father attempted to flog him, he would run a dirk-knife through him. He produced the dirk, and said he had bought it on purpose. I begged of him not to think of such a thing. He swore he would; and the next time his master was going to whip him, he pulled out the dirk, and ran through the house. His father sold him soon after this. I saw him afterwards. He had been sold to a hatter, and a smarter or more gentlemanly-looking young fellow I have rarely seen. He said, "Oh, Francis, I am so glad that you persuaded me not to kill my master. I have got a good master now, and, if not sold, I shall be happy." That which in my own case weighed most heavily upon my mind was the thought that all my work was for another; and that even the flesh and blood, the bone and sinew, which God had given me, I could not call my own. I never had parted with them, but another called them his. Heaven will, no doubt, in its own good time, redress this shameless, cruel, infamous wrong.

CHAPTER IV.

Corn Songs in Harvest-time—Conversion.

In harvest-time, thirty or forty years ago, it was customary to give the slaves a good deal of grog, the masters thinking that the slaves could not do the hard work without the spirits. A great change has taken place now in this respect; many of the planters during harvest give their slaves sixpence a day instead of the whiskey. The consequence is there is not a fifth of the sickness there was some years ago. The country is intensely hot in the harvest-time, and those who drank grog would then want water; and, having got water, they would want grog again; consequently, they soon either were sick or drunk. All round where I dwelt the sixpence was generally substituted for the spirits; the slaves are looking better, and there are fewer outbreaks in the fields. In the autumn, about the 1st of November, the slaves commence gathering the Indian-corn, pulling it off the stalk, and throwing it into heaps. Then it is carted home, and thrown into heaps sixty or seventy yards long, seven or eight feet high, and about six or seven feet wide. Some of the masters make their slaves shuck the corn. All the slaves stand on one side of the heap, and throw the ears over, which are then cribbed. This is the time when the whole country far and wide resounds with the corn-songs. When they commence shucking the corn, the master will say, "Ain't you going to sing any to-night?" The slaves say, "Yers, Sir." One slave will begin:—

> "Fare you well, Miss Lucy.
> ALL. John come down de hollow."

The next song will be:—

> "Fare you well, fare you well.
> ALL. Weell ho. Weell ho.
> CAPTAIN. Fare you well, young ladies all.
> ALL. Weell. ho. Weell ho.
> CAPTAIN. Fare you well, I'm going away.
> ALL. Weell ho. Weell ho.
> CAPTAIN. I'm going away to Canada.
> ALL. Weell ho. Weell ho."

One night Mr. Taylor, a large planter,[36] had a corn shucking, a Bee it is called.[37] The corn pile was 180 yards long. He sent his slaves on horseback with letters to the other planters around to ask them to allow their slaves to come and help. On a Thursday night, about 8 o'clock, the slaves were heard coming, the corn-songs ringing through the plantations. "Oh, they are coming, they are coming!" exclaimed Mr. Taylor, who had been anxiously listening some time for the songs. The slaves marched up in companies, headed by captains, who had in the crowns of their hats a short stick, with feathers tied to it, like a cockade. I myself was in one of the companies. Mr. Taylor shook hands with each captain as the companies arrived, and said the men were to have some brandy if they wished, a large jug of which was ready for them. Mr. Taylor ordered the corn-

36. The 1850 and 1860 census and slave schedules for Kentucky list a Jesse Taylor as a farmer and owner of a large estate (valued in 1850 at $13,000) in Mason County.

37. For a similar description of a Kentucky corn-husking bee employing two competing teams, see Harry Smith, *Fifty Years in Slavery in the United States of America* (Grand Rapids: West Michigan Printing Co., 1891), 62. See also *The Autobiography of Elder Madison Campbell, Pastor of the United Colored Baptist Church, Richmond, Kentucky* (Richmond, Ky.: Pantagraph Job Rooms, 1895). Campbell recalls the corn songs heard at Kentucky corn-shucking bees during his youth. He describes how the slaves chose a "general of the corn pile" who lined out songs as the men shucked a long row of corn. The general sang that he

> Got a letter from Tennessee
> That the Queen of Morocco had wrote to me
> That the Negroes were all going to be free.

(69–70)

pile to be divided into two by a large pole laid across. Two men were chosen as captains; and the men, to the number of 300 or 400, were told off to each captain. One of the captains got Mr. Taylor on his side, who said he should not like his party to be beaten. "Don't throw the corn too far. Let some of it drop just over, and we'll shingle some,[38] and get done first. I can make my slaves shuck what we shingle tomorrow," said Mr. Taylor, "for I hate to be beaten."

The corn-songs now rang out merrily; all working willingly and gaily. Just before they had finished the heaps, Mr. Taylor went away into the house; then the slaves, on Mr. Taylor's side, by shingling, beat the other side; and his Captain, and all his men, rallied around the others, and took their hats in their hands, and cried out, "Oh, oh! fie! for shame!"

It was two o'clock in the morning now, and they marched to Mr. Taylor's house; the Captain hollering out, "Oh, where's Mr. Taylor? Oh, where's Mr. Taylor?" all the men answering, "Oh, oh, oh!" Mr. Taylor walked, with all his family, on the verandah; and the Captain sang,

> I've just come to let you know.
> MEN. Oh, oh, oh!
> CAPTAIN. The upper end has beat.
> MEN. Oh, oh, oh!
> CAPTAIN. But isn't they sorry fellows?
> MEN. Oh, oh, oh!
> CAPTAIN. But isn't they sorry fellows?
> MEN. Oh, oh, oh!
> CAPTAIN. But I'm going back again,
> MEN. Oh, oh, oh!
> CAPTAIN. But I'm going back again.
> MEN. Oh, oh, oh!
> CAPTAIN. And where's Mr. Taylor?
> MEN. Oh, oh, oh!
> CAPTAIN. And where's Mr. Taylor?

38. The meaning of "shingle" here is not clear. It may refer to stacking the corn in overlapping formation like the tiles on a roof.

MEN. Oh, oh, oh!
CAPTAIN. And where's Mrs. Taylor?
MEN. Oh, oh, oh!
CAPTAIN. I'll bid you, fare you well,
MEN. Oh, oh, oh!
CAPTAIN. For I'm going back again.
MEN. Oh, oh, oh!
CAPTAIN. I'll bid you, fare you well,
And a long fare you well.
MEN. Oh, oh, oh!

They marched back, and finished the pile. All then went to enjoy a good supper, provided by Mr. Taylor, it being usual to kill an ox on such an occasion; Mr., Mrs., and the Misses Taylor, waiting upon the slaves, at supper. What I have written cannot convey a tenth part of the spirit, humour, and mirth of the company; all joyous—singing, coming and going.

But, within one short fortnight, at least thirty of this happy band were sold, many of them down South, to unutterable horrors, soon to be used up. Reuben, the merry Captain of the band, a fine, spirited fellow, who sang, "Where's Mr. Taylor?" was one of those, dragged from his family. My heart is full when I think of his sad lot.

Conversion.

One day, when I was between twenty-five and thirty years of age, an elderly lady, who was on a visit to my mistress, came into the kitchen, and, after speaking to me about things in general for a short time, she took a Bible out of her pocket, and said, "Would you like to hear me read something about our Lord and Saviour Jesus Christ?" I said, "Please, marm." She said, "If your mistress should get to know that I have been reading to you, she would be very angry, and drive me from the house." She then read that portion of Scripture, where it says, "All that forget God shall be turned into hell." There was such an evident sincerity about the good old lady, and her manner was so kind, that every word which she either read or spoke to me went to my heart. Here was truth presented to me, by one whose only possible object could be to do me good.

I listened eagerly to every word which fell from her lips. She told me, if I believed in the Lord Jesus Christ, I should be saved; that God was no respecter of persons; that He loved all His people, black as well as white. She told me, if I loved God, and showed it by my conduct, He would love me, and at last take me to heaven to live with Him; that the Gospel was commanded, by our Saviour, to be preached to all people; and that He died for the sins of all men, that they, through Him, might be saved. And many such encouraging passages, she either quoted, or gave me the substance of. She promised that, when she came again, she would give me a spelling-book.

She said, "I know you are allowed to go to the chapel, but there the preachers only preach what will be agreeable to your masters. The real naked truth of the Gospel, the glad tidings that were intended to comfort all hearts, you never hear."

All this conversation was carried on in a secret manner, lest my master or mistress should have the slightest hint of any such thing.

At night, I turned over in my mind every word which had been said; and I resolved, from that time forward, to put my trust in God, and get to know as much as I possibly could about Jesus Christ.

The good lady, true to her promise, brought me the spelling-book, and told me to lay it aside, and when she came again, she would teach me one word at a time. I put it into the pastry-room, where my mistress's sister found it. She asked me what I was doing with such a book? She said for one cent she would break my head with it; and that she would make my master give me one hundred lashes, if she ever knew me to have another.

When the good lady who had given me the book learnt what had been done and said about it, she was very much grieved, and said she was truly sorry that the Bible should be kept a sealed book from the poor benighted heathen.

Kind readers, you who have been anxious to send your missionaries to the East and the West, to the North and the South, to men of every nation and race, what can be your opinion of those who deliberately keep millions of men in the grossest ignorance? It cannot be pretended for one moment, truthfully, that we are not capable of understanding if we were taught. I myself am a living witness against such an absurdity; after fifty years of age I have learnt to read and write. No, no. It is not our stupidity, but the slaveowners' lust for power and gain which makes them directly oppose the precepts of our Lord and His apostles to teach all to search the Scriptures. It is only by keeping the poor slaves in brutish ignorance that they can uphold slavery. Let the slaves have the same opportunity as the freemen to learn to read and write, and nothing could prevent their rising and freeing themselves. But I would have my readers mark the effect of the accursed system even upon the gentle nature of woman. Imagine any lady in this country threatening 100 lashes because a poor servant was found trying to read; why the whole country would ring with the brutality of such a thing.

The kind lady who gave me the spelling-book removed to Lexington, and I never saw her again; but her words of sympathy and goodness will abide with me as long as life lasts. But Providence, who had by her hands sown the good seed, soon sent another friend to nurture it, and endeavour to bring it to maturity. A planter, a truly Christian gentleman, a neighbour of my master's, saw me standing by the road-side one Sunday. "Come to my house this evening," he said. I replied; "Yes, Sir"; but I was not aware what he wanted me for. When it was dark, that very evening, I went to his house. "Does your master know that you have come?" he said. "No, Sir," I answered. "I am glad of that," he said, "he would be annoyed if he knew what I wanted with you. I wish to speak to you about your soul." He put several questions to me concerning religion; but he soon discovered by my answers that I was relying too much upon myself and upon works. He read the words to me, "Believe in the Lord Jesus Christ, and thou shalt be saved, thou and thy house."

What the gentleman said to me made me very anxious about religion, and about my salvation. I was very distressed in my mind, and the next night I went from the house of my master down into a valley to pray, and to think about heaven and everything which had been read to me. Oh, how I longed for the Lord to change my heart, and make me fit for

His heavenly kingdom. I came to a spot in the vale where the roots of the trees protruded some distance out of the ground. I bruised my knees against these, thinking that the Lord would the sooner convert me, out of pity for the way in which I had hurt myself. I prayed earnestly in the best way I could to God to enlighten my mind and to save me. I went in the course of a few days to the kind planter, and told him all I thought and felt, and showed him how I had bruised my knees. He told me that the Lord looked at the heart, and wished that to be changed, that self-mortifications and cuttings and woundings were what the heathens did to propitiate their false gods, but that a broken and a contrite heart was alone acceptable to God. That I was not to put my faith in works, but in the Lord Jesus our Saviour. Thus it was that I came to a true knowledge of the Almighty and of religion. Through many and many a trial, and in deep suffering and anguish, both of body and mind, what I learnt from this good man has been a source of comfort to me. The weary burden of slavery has been lightened by it, my days of freedom are rejoiced by it, and to it as to an anchor I hope to hold fast until the closing scenes of life.

CHAPTER V.

The slaveholders, as a body, are very superstitious, and are continually haunted with fears of ghosts and goblins. No one ought, therefore, to wonder at the poor ignorant slave being imbued with fear of what he considers supernatural; but an anecdote, which I have omitted to relate, will best illustrate what I mean.

Superstition of the Slaveholders.

It was a common practice among our slave-women to say to their children, if they shouted out, "Ole boy, I'll pully your ears!" the old boy would answer, "Ha! ha! Ha!" You might often, therefore, hear the children calling out these words in the fields in their play. One day when they were returning from the bush, crying out, "Ole boy, I'll pully your ears!" I got behind a large hogshead, and cried out as dismally as I could, prolonging the sound through my hands, "Ha! ha! ha! Ha! ha! Ha!" They instantly ran with all their might, shouting, "We didé hear someting, we didé hear someting." They after a few minutes, as if to assure themselves, returned, calling the same words again, "Ole boy, I'll pully your ears," and I gave the same reply as before, "Ha! Ha! ha!" They scampered off as quickly as their legs would carry them, half frightened to death. I looked round the hogshead, and saw them running towards my master's house, and then observed them standing by him, as if telling him, and then the horn gave three or four quick blasts for all hands to return from the fields. Soon I saw the slaves hastening towards the house, and my master motioning to the women to come from the spinning-rooms, and calling out all his own family. He then, with the children in front, came towards where I was, and I heard him say to the children, "Whereabouts do you think, he was when you heard him answer?" They said, "We no ideah yet, its waysh, uppé yonder." He said, "When near the place you must holla again." So very soon they hollered again, "Ole boy, I'll pully your ears." Then I shouted as loudly as I could, "Ha—a—a," and I heard a tremendous running and screaming, "Oh, Lord! oh, Lord!" some tumbling over one another. In about five minutes I heard them talking and returning, and my master asking the slaves if they did not hear something; the slaves said they did, and my mistress said she was sure she did. "Well," thought I, "if you didn't you shall; only holla again." He told the children to cry out again, and this time, with all my might, like some wild beast, I replied, "U—U—U—h!" and men, women, and children, hand over head, scrambling in terror, ran back, evidently nearly out of their senses. I kept quiet some time, and then secretly hastened to the cabin. My mistress was laid up some days from the combined effects of fear and running. The devil was now known to be at hand.

After this, I never in my life saw such a change as there was on my master's plantation; he spoke to every one so kindly, and went about crying, "Oh, what shall I do, what shall I do? I heard the Old Boy, I did, I did!" and crying, "O Lord, O Lord, don't let him take us; oh, don't, oh, don't!" He called out to my uncle on the Saturday, about two o'clock, when the slaves were coming out of their cabins from dinner, "My good fellow, my good fellow!" in a most piteous tone, "come here! come here! I hope you all have had plenty of dinner; I told the missis to give more meat; I hope you all have had enough!" "Yers, sir, yers, sir," the slaves said; "we have enough to-day, we have enough to-day." He, in the utmost anguish of tone and manner, said, "Because I want you all to have enough; to be better fed and not to work so hard. Oh, Lord! oh, Lord!" Crying, he said, "You know to-day is Saturday." My uncle said, "Yers, sir, to-day is Saturday." "Go and make all the hands get their wood chopped for Sunday: they must not do any work on Sunday. Let the slaves get all their chores[39]

39. Original version has "chose."

done, for there must be no work done on Sunday. We heard the old boy answer the other day. He is coming to take us all away." And he cried like a child, "What shall I do! what shall I do! what shall I do! Oh dear! oh dear! oh dear!" When my mistress was well, after the fright and the running, I have every reason to believe, from what I had heard said, that my master would have liberated all his slaves; but, boy-like, I could not keep the secret, and told one of the slaves how cleverly I had acted the Ole Boy, behind the hogshead, and frightened them all. The woman went and told my mistress that it was Francis. My mistress laughed and cried too, and said, "What will be done with that little nigger?" She told my master about it, and he declared he would whip me to death. He sent for me to come to the house; he stood with the raw cow's hide, and said, brandishing the whip, "You little nigger, I will whip the life out of you." I danced about and screamed, "I won't do it again!" Raising the lash, he said, "I'll take good care you don't; I'll kill you, you little nigger!" My mistress begged so hard, "Oh, don't! oh, don't! he is too little," and so I escaped. In two or three months' time all the effects had vanished, and Satan's kingdom was worse than ever through the whole plantation; it was a regular torment, and I was made the most wretched being imaginable, all the slaves blaming me because they were so cruelly treated, saying I had told the secret and brought misery again upon them all. It was a common saying for the slaves months after, "Massa's gone back to de begging[40] elements of de world."

The Negroes' Party.

Among the American planters there are some of a kind, humane, and generous nature, who do everything they possibly can to mitigate the evils of slavery. But, however strange it may appear, these are the greatest supports to the system. Indeed, if it were not for these bright exceptions shedding a humanizing light upon the unspeakable evils of slavery, the world would long ago have been so horrified by it, that it must

---

40. Perhaps this is a mistranscription for "beginning."

have been rooted out. If all were bad, and acted as the majority do, with the greatest severity and brutality, we should not hear persons palliating this enforced servitude by arguments drawn from the conduct of a few. I knew a gentleman, a planter, whose name and merits I wish to hold in remembrance, a Mr. Franklin, having above a hundred slaves, cultivating chiefly tobacco and hemp in Kentucky. He was a bachelor. His overseer was Thomas, a black man, who had some portion of his master's kindness about him in managing the estate. His housekeeper, Thomas's wife, Sookey, looked after the household matters in somewhat of the same spirit. To these two were entrusted the entire management of everything during the absence from home of Mr. Franklin, which frequently was for three or four months at a time.

He had often heard his neighbours say, "Why, Mr. Franklin, when you are from home, there are pretty doings at your house. The place is full of niggers, and Thomas and Sookey carry on a nice game, treating all hands." Mr. Franklin was resolved to find out for himself exactly the state of affairs. So calling Thomas and Sookey to him, he told them it was his intention to go from home for three or four months, and ordered them to get his things ready for the journey. His clothes were duly packed up by Sookey, and his horse was brought out ready harnessed by Thomas. But Mr. Franklin had secretly put away his clothes in a drawer, and had adroitly substituted the oldest and most ragged things he could lay his hands on, not forgetting a battered old hat. On his supposed journey he started. Early in the evening Sookey sent the slaves round to announce that her master had gone from home, and that a party was to assemble that evening. Not fewer than forty or fifty, when it was dark, hastened to Mr. Franklin's house to enjoy themselves of the best which Sookey could provide. The parlour and the drawing-room were quickly filled with men and women eagerly bent upon pleasure. Their conversation was of the most animated description,—about how many lashes one had received because the apportioned work had not been done; how many cuts another had to spin and reel off; how one had cunningly escaped, and another had been lashed. About half-past eleven at night a knock was heard at the door; an old white beggar begged to be allowed to enter and warm himself. Sookey, with a large turban on her head, stepped forward and asked what he wanted. "Oh no," she said, "you can't come in to-night, I have got a party of friends here; certainly not." Her husband Thomas came at this moment to the door, dressed in the best suit that was left at home, and, with his fingers in the waistcoat arm-holes, and drawing himself up, "Oh! let poor beggar come in," he said. "Come in and warm yourself." In hobbled the poor benighted beggar, and took his seat by the fire. Some of the party now came into the kitchen, and peering at him, "Aunt Sookey, where did that old beggar come from?" one would say. "See here, old beggar man, where you live?" The beggar, in a low tone, replied, "Don't live far from here." One of the women, taking hold of her petticoats, and gliding up to him, said, "Old beggar man, dese de best close you got?" "Yers, marm," he said. "Old beggar, if we didn't give all our workey for noting, we give you better clothes. We get noting for work, massa gets all. Beggar man! you got any slaves?" she said. "No, I've got no slaves." "Would you have any if you was able to buy 'em?" "Well," he said, "if I had 'em I would treat 'em well." The woman said, "But if you get into debt, wouldn't you sell 'em?" He said, "I'm too poor to talk about owning anything." The women having hold of the men's arms with one hand, and their gowns with the other, walked past the poor old man with all the airs of duchesses, making various remarks as they went by.

One of Mr. Franklin's slaves said to another slave, "If me was as old as Methioseleh, me wouldn't run away, massa, be so good." One of the black maids had taken a dress of her young mistress out of the drawer to show off in this night, when, as bad luck would have it, one of the men accidentally trod upon it, and rent it up; dire was the distress and confusion, and the endeavouring to mend it, lest the mishap should be discovered. "My massa," said one of the slaves, "aint very good massa. I's going to run away, de first chance I get, to Canada, I tell you; I's going to leave him." Another said, "What for?" "Why, because I know when he gets in debt he go sell me, sure as you born." The other replied, "No, he aint going sell you." Then all the slaves cried out together, "I wish somebody would knock dat nigger in de head. Now, don't you hear im say dat massa wouldn't sell im when he gets in debt? Eberybody know better en dat."

Now, cheered by the best drink which the establishment could afford, many were the knowing remarks which they made concerning the qualities of the liquors. "Dis is de best brandy dat I ever did drink in my life." "Well, I don't know about dat, jus give me some of de old gin, dat is as good as anyting." "Jus give me some of dat ole rye whisky, and dat is jus all I want"; each speaking according to his taste or fancy. One said, "Well, I must go and see arter dis old beggaroowe. Come, now, ole beggar man," he said, "I want you to be getting out o' dis," reeling one step forward, and two back, having got pretty well drunk. One of the women said, "Oh, no, now jus let dat ole beggar man alone. He must have someting to eat and drink afore he go away, because," she said, "now who knows but dat ole beggar may get up in de world some day, and we be sold, an' he buy some of us in de slave-market, and treat us well for dis— one good turn deserves anoder; and so I aint going to have dat beggar man run upon here tonight."

When the supper was all laid, the women, having hold of the arms of the men, walked with all the consequence, and imitating all the manners of their mistresses, into the dining-room, and seated themselves at the tables. The supper had been delayed for some time, because four or five of the young women who were waiting-maids refused to enter the dining-room, being indignant at the thought that the old beggar was to sit along with them. However, the difficulty was got over by the old woman who took an interest in the beggar saying there was nothing like peace, and she would send something into the kitchen to him, "and den," she said, "he should come to de table when we genfolks[41] had done." While they were taking supper, Nelly said, "Me send someting into ole beggar man, since he get hungry, we genfolks sitting chatting so long." One of the women seized Nelly by her arm, who was reaching to put some pound cake on the plate for the old beggar. "You shan't," she said, "you make youself very busy about dat beggar. You an im, too, will go out faster den you come in, if you don't mine." The grace before meat was, "Lord, bless dat good massa of Thomas and Sookey, dat managed so well to leave so

41. I.e., "gentlefolks."

many good tings to set before us, and hoping dat he turn home all right";
and they all responded, "A-men, A-men."

After they had eaten a little, the conversation began afresh. "There
ain't such a nice lady in de country as my missis," said one. Another disputed eagerly with her, saying that "her missis was as good, if not better,"
all who were kindly treated praising their mistresses as unequalled. One
young man protested that his young master knew more than any young
gentleman he ever saw in his life, "because," he said, "my young massa
is going to get married in two or three weeks. Now, how do you tink
he got his wife? Why, because a young lady was praising his hoss, and
he said, 'How would you like its massa?' and dat de way de work commenced; and she might have praised all de gemmen's hosses in de country, and none would have made de answer; because my Massa has got
more approbranchen (apprehension)[42] den all de gemmens in de country." "My Massa," said another, "he whip me ebery time I go away from
home without asking im, and de next new moon I going to make way to
Great Britain's land, to Canada, jus as sure as you born." Another said,
"If I had such a massa as Mr. Franklin, uncle Thomas and aunt Sookey's massa, den I tink myself well off." Another said, "I see jus as good
a massa in de country as Mr. Franklin, and when he got into debt he sold
all his slaves." And all the company; cried out to this observation, "True,
true." Some of them said, "We couldn't be no happier if it wasn't for selling." One said, "You see de hen in de morning got twelve chickens, and
before night de hawk take dem all away but five"; and she said, "Brethren, though we be enjoying ourselves to-night, before de end of de week
some of us may be sold down de river." And all said, "True, true, true.
My God!" One of the women said, "My massa and missis very kind, but
my massa get into debt, and I see him dodging away from de sheriffs dis
two months, and he gone and sold all his hemp and tobacco, and den he
gone and sold all de wheat, and so he sold all his fat pigs and three or
four beeves, and I hear my fellow-servant, de waiter, he say dat he habent
half de debt paid; so every morning I get down on my knees and kiss all

42. The word intended is presumably not "apprehension," as Fedric's scribe inserts
parenthetically, but "approbation."

my little chilun before I go into de fields because dey might sell me in de field, and I mightn't come back home to see dem no more." And many said they had witnessed the same thing. And many a one said, "Jus give me my freedom, and pay me for my work, and I work for my massa from daylight till dark. I wouldn't leave my plantation to go nowhere else if me jus had my freedom, so, I wouldn't be sold away from my family. I lub my wife and chilun." And one old woman said, "I says so too, because de worst whipping I ever had in all my life was because I cried when dey sold my son, and dey would have sold me, but when dey stripped my shoulders at de market, I was whipped so bad dey said dey wouldn't hab me." Aunt Lucy said, "Now, uncle Harry, you say you a Christian man." He said, "Yers, I do, I trust I am a Christian." "Massa last week," Lucy said, "whipt my back awful because I went to a prayer-meeting. He say, 'Why don't you ask me?' But when I ask he won't let me go, and I see im since he whipt me take de Lord's-supper. I was sitting in de gallery looking at im. To see de oaths coming out of his mouth when he was whipping me, and den to see him sitting dare and taking de Lord's-supper, I had to turn my head away and not look at im. Now, uncle Harry, what do you tink of im?" Uncle Harry said, "Well, Lucy, if it's true what you say, hell is full of such Christians."

Aunt Amy came up, and began to tell about her master whipping her because she had not done her task in spinning. Fanny and Melvey said, "Now, uncle Harry, hear what we have got to say. Half de times dat aunt Amy gets whipt it be her own fault. 'Cause when her massa calls her 'You ugly old devil,' for all she knows dare ain't an uglier white man in all Kentucky dan he is, she talks right back to im, and she say, 'I have seen cleverer gemmens dan you.' What can she expect when she insult im?" Several of the slaves spoke up and said, "Amy was wrong in talking back, dey could not expect noting else from dare massas." Humphery said, "Dat ole beggar will tell what you all be talking about; I tell you, he sits dare listening." Somebody said, "For Lor sake let de ole beggar alone, for de white folks as good as de black folks, as long dey behave demselves."

Mimey said, "Well, uncle Harry, my missis is not a good missis; she was up in de garret to-day, and dat is as near heben as she ever will get. I will give de debble his due, she do chain de debble up all day Sunday, but she let im out on de Monday morning." Billy said, "Well, uncle Harry, what do you say about all dese bad white folks?" Uncle Harry said, "Well, I want you all to be good; you be talking so much about your bad massas, and I hab been telling you all dis long time about your duty to be good Christians." Billy said, "Well, if my massa was as good man as I believe you are, I could be a good man; but he say he be Christian, and he does such tings as I wouldn't do. He seem to stand right before me, he seem to get right in my way. I tink if my massa die de way he is now, de debble would have him, he worse den de debble." Up came Dinah and Grace, and said, "Well, uncle Harry, I know dat we have lost four slave-holders dat I don't tink de debble would put em wid de rest. He must hab some place to put em by demselves, dey so bad he wouldn't put em wid de rest." It was decided by two-thirds of the company that 'the debil was but a debil,' but that their masters professed to be Christians, and yet their acts made them worse than the devil.

Cupid, a smart nigger, a waiter, with his hands under his coat-tails, strutted up to the beggar, and said, "How dare you to come here to-night, where dere is ladies and gemmens, with such clothes as dese on? Now, you must never be catched doing such a ting again. Now," said Cupid, standing before him with one hand under his coat-tails, and motioning with the other, "you may always know, from dis time for ever, dat de black folks are de best folks, 'cause you see now we allow you to sit now where dere is ladies and gemmens, and you are not taken by de pole of your neck and throwed out of doors, as de white people would do wid one of us if we was to come into such a party with such rags." Then Cupid, placing his fingers in his waistcoat armholes, bowing to the beggar, said, "Well, you are a very civil ole fellow, after all; won't you hab a glass of someting to drink?" "Yes, please," answered the beggar. Cupid poured out a glass of brandy, and walked up to him, "Here, take dis, you are [a] good ole fellow, after all." Uncle Harry said, "I want you all to pray and ask de Lord to give us all such massas as Thomas and Sookey's massa, dat we may hab some more places to get such good things to eat. And now I wish you all to rise." And they all rose up, and he said, "In the midst of slavery dere is something to be thankful for. To-night, we are blessed to have good food given. Oh, Lord, make us thankful, and bless de good massa of dis house." And all said, "Amen, amen."

The beggar was now called into the dining-room, and Aunt Sookey gave him some of the good things. He then went and sat down by the fire again. It happened that two or three years before this Mr. Franklin had been helping the men to chop some firewood, and he had cut his foot very badly. Aunt Sookey had attended to the wound. After it was well, there was still a large scar on the foot. The old beggar by the fire began to pull off his shoe and sock. His foot was stretched out. Aunt Sookey, coming to the fire, said, "I wish you would be getting ready to go away. You needn't be pulling off your shoe; you ain't going to stop here." She looked steadfastly at the foot for a few moments, and then, stepping backwards and coming forwards again, repeating these movements three or four times, as if some dreadful thought had seized her, she said, "Tommy, Tommy, Tommy!" "What, what?" he said. She said, "Come here, come here! Don't you tink dat massa Johnny's foot?"[43] Uncle Tommy, taking her by the shoulders and turning her round, said, "Oh, you go away." Then he walked towards the beggar's foot, looking anxiously at it, and starting affrighted back; and then stepped forward again, as if to make himself sure of something, and then ran back again terrified, and cried out, "It is massa Johnny's foot. It is, it is massa Johnny's foot." And Aunt Sookey shouted out, "Oh, oh!" and ran away, she out of one door, and he out of the other. Now ensued a scene of indescribable confusion. The first hat that any one could seize he put on his head and ran off. In one minute

43. Similarities between this episode and the scene in the *Odyssey* where Odysseus returns secretly to Ithaca, his home, disguised as a beggar, and is recognized by one of his servants because of the scar on his leg, have led some readers to discount the whole narrative as fiction. While it is possible that Fedric or his scribe may have embellished this episode along the lines of the *Odyssey* incident, it is also quite possible that Franklin himself was inspired to imitate Odysseus and/or that he could be identified by just such a scar.

all had disappeared; and, what surprised me the most, was that, although five minutes before several men were staggering drunk, not one found the slightest difficulty in understanding the nature of the discovery, and scampering off as nimbly as if he had not tasted a drop.

The old white beggar, changed to be Mr. Franklin, the master of the establishment, called to his ostler, and ordered him to go into the woodland pasture, and directed him where he would find his horse and gig fastened up to a tree, and told him to bring it to the house. Another slave he ordered to call Thomas and Sookey, and tell them to come in and put everything away and he would not disturb them. When the servant went to call them in, and told them what their master said, they came in, and Mr. Franklin called Aunt Sookey, saying, "Sookey, come here." Sookey entered the room, and began to beg his pardon. He said, "I only want you to get me some clothes to put on. You shall not hear anything more about it." Uncle Thomas wished to come in to beg his pardon. Aunt Sookey told Mr. Franklin that Thomas wanted to beg his pardon, and he said, "Tell Thomas to get on putting things away. There will be nothing more about it."

In about five or six weeks afterwards I saw Aunt Sookey, and asked her if Mr. Franklin had ever whipped her and Uncle Thomas about the spree. She said, "No"; and she told me how, when all had gone, Mr. Franklin had acted kindly. She said she had heard her master say to a gentleman that he had been to a good many theatres, but he never in his life was at one where he had so enjoyed himself as at the Niggers' Spree. He said if some of the black women had had white faces, he should have thought it was their mistresses, their manners and demeanour being exact copies of the white ladies; and Sookey told me that Mr. Franklin said, "Indeed, he never could have believed it if he had not seen it." He said (evidently alluding to the kind attention he had received from Nelly) that "certainly in woman's nature there was the milk of human kindness." I hope that no debt or other misfortune has compelled this good man to part with any of his slaves, or assuredly they will find a difference elsewhere.

CHAPTER VI.

Labour of any kind despised—Slaves the Badge of Distinction among Planters—Impudence of the Ladies.

A contempt for workers characterizes every one in any way connected with slavery. Nothing seems so degrading to them as to do the slightest menial office, such as making a pie, or tart, or any little article of cooking. They talk generally about doing such things as a person in England would talk about a gentleman dragging a cart, or a lady carrying a basket upon her head. Slaves do everything; and I have often heard the ladies say, when they had been to the North, that they were pleased they had returned home, as they hated to be waited upon by white folks.

Slaves the Badge of Distinction among Planters.

The principal badge of distinction among the Southerners in America is the possession of slaves. A very nice young gentleman, whose father had no slaves, but yet was wealthy, came to pay his addresses to a young lady of similar fortune to his own. She wished him to discontinue his visits, since his father, she said, had not the toenail of a nigger in the world. She said to her footman, "Vincent, I wish you could play some trick upon him, so that he would not come again." "I can do it nicely," said Vincent. "I shall consider you a clever fellow if you can," she said; "and I will make you a present if you do." When the gentleman came again, Vincent had ready a piece of shoemaker's wax, flattened out thin, and, holding with his right hand the gentleman's horse whilst he was going to mount, he slipped with his left the piece of wax on to the saddle. The gentleman rode home, but when the servant came to take the horse, he found his master could not dismount, and ran into the house and told the family that his young master could not get off his horse. They all came on the verandah, and asked him what was the matter. He said "he did not know, but he was fast to the saddle." After considerable difficulty, amidst a good deal of laughter, he was separated from the saddle, his father saying, "I would advise you to stay at home another time, since you may see that you are not wanted where you have been."

This kind of practical joke is very common among the Southern young ladies. Their black footmen are prompted to pass them off upon young gentlemen whose fathers are not slaveholders. Hence, if a young gentleman should politely take the reins of a horse to assist the lady to mount, the footman would hold fast and saucily say, "I come for dis purpose." The gentleman, looking in the laughing face of the lady, would perceive in an instant that he was not wanted, and walk away directly.

CHAPTER VII.

First Attempt to Escape—Pursued by Bloodhounds—Reach Bear's Wallow,
a Dismal Swamp—Conceal myself in a Cavern—Driven by hunger,
give myself up to my Master—Receive 107 Lashes—Brutally
treated afterwards by my Master.

Work, work, work, one day like another, only I had now been to several prayer-meetings, and had got a knowledge of religion, which comforted me. I thought about the future, when I should be free from my master, when I could join in psalms and hymns and prayers without being afraid of the lash. Such consolation and joy did I receive from these meetings, that I have run the risk over and over again of being flogged for attending them. Thus one weary day, and week, and month, and year passed on with me being turned out of the kitchen sometimes, when my master was in his drunken fits, to work in the fields.

I had been flogged for going to a prayer-meeting, and, before my back was well, my master was going to whip me again. I determined, therefore, to run away. It was in the morning, just after my master had got his breakfast, I was ordered to the back of the premises to strip. My master had got the thong of raw cow's hide when off I ran, towards the swamp.

Pursued by Bloodhounds.

He saw me running, and instantly called three bloodhounds, kept for the purpose, and put them on my track. I saw them coming up to me, when, turning round to them, I clapped my hands, and called them by name; for I had been in the habit of feeding them. I urged them on, as if in pursuit of something else. They instantly passed me, and flew upon the cattle. I saw my master calling them off, and returning. No doubt, he perceived it was useless to pursue me with dogs which knew me so well.

Reach Bear's Wallow, a dismal Swamp.[44]

I now hurried on further, into a dismal swamp named the Bear's Wallow; and, at last, wearied and exhausted, I sat down at the foot of a tree to rest, and think what had best be done.

I knelt down, and prayed earnestly to the Almighty, to protect and direct me what to do. I rose from my knees, and looked stealthily around, afraid that the dogs and men were still in pursuit. I listened, and listened again, to the slightest sound, made by the flapping of the wings of a bird, or the rustling of the wild animals among the underwood; and then proceeded further into the swamp. My path was interrupted every now and then by large sheets of stagnant, putrid, green-looking water, from which a most sickening, fetid smell arose; the birds, in their flight, turning away from it. The snakes crawled sluggishly across the ground, for it was autumn time, when, it is said, they are surcharged with their deadly poison. Their tameness frightened me, as I stood admiring their various hues, and immense coils. A kind Providence seemed to have made them harmless to me, for they never bit or molested me.

Conceal myself in a Cavern.

I came, at length, to an overhanging rock, forming a species of natural cavern, into which I crept to rest me. I was footsore, and torn by the thorns, and parched with thirst. After a short time, I crept out to pluck some berries to quench my thirst, and then re-entered the cavern, to lie for the night. But the barking of the wild dogs, the growling of the bears,

44. The area Fedric refers to is presumably near the road in southeastern Mason County now called Bear's Wallow Road, approximately fifteen miles from Maysville. The swamp, where bears used to immerse themselves in the mud and water, no longer exists, but there is still a large pond near the intersection of North and South Bear's Wallow Road and Polecat Pike, and there is also a large marshy area toward the end of North Bear's Wallow Road, bordered by low hills and forest.

and sounds of wild animals of various kinds, made me start from my feverish sleep. When awake in the morning, I tried to plan out some way of escape over the Ohio River, which I knew was about thirty miles from where I was. But I could not swim; and I was well aware that my master would set a watch upon every ferry or ford, and that the whole country would be put on the alert to catch me; for the planters, for self-protection, take almost as much interest in capturing another man's slaves, as they do their own.[45]

I walked for some distance round about the cavern, having determined to make it my place of abode until I could hit upon some plan of escape. I was in continual fear when I plucked the berries to eat them, lest I should be poisoned; for I had known that slaves, especially children, had been killed by eating some kinds of wild berries. Sometimes I vomited very much after eating some; at other times those which I plucked agreed with me better. But I am unable to describe the difference of the berries in other respects.

I came, several times, near to dead polecats, the stench from which was dreadful, and in my weak state produced sickness. One day and night were very much like another, except that I occasionally heard the noise of men and dogs—no doubt, in pursuit of other negroes. My mind whenever I heard the barking of dogs was distressed beyond all description. I felt sure, until the sounds ceased, that they would scent me out, and strange dogs would have torn me to pieces, the masters preferring their slaves to be devoured rather than to allow them to escape.

45. See footnote 27 above for confirmation that slave owners formed societies whose purpose was to aid one another in recapturing runaway slaves. On November 23, 1852, the *Louisville Courier* reported that slave holders from Mason and adjoining counties had held a meeting "for the purpose of devising means to better secure the slave property of Kentucky." Those attending the meeting urged "the formation of slave protection societies in each county of the state, especially those bordering the Ohio," and the establishment of a pursuing committee in each city financed to cover the expenses of the pursuit and the payment of rewards (quoted in J. Blaine Hudson, *Fugitive Slaves and the Underground Railroad in the Kentucky Borderland* [Jefferson, NC: McFarlane & Co., 2002], 14). Hudson estimates that from 1830 to 1860 between 1,100 and 1,200 slaves attempted to escape each year, and that approximately half of the would-be escapees were recaptured.

At length, driven by hunger and desperation, I approached the edge of the swamp, when I was startled by seeing a young woman ploughing. I knew her and called her by name. She was frightened, and shocked at my appearance—worn from hunger almost to a skeleton, and haggard from the want of sound sleep. I begged of her to go to get me something to eat. She, at first, expressed her fears, and began to tell me of the efforts which my master was making to capture me. He had offered 500 dollars' reward—had placed a watch all along the Ohio River—had informed all the neighbouring planters, who had cautioned all their slaves not to give me any food or other assistance,—and he had made it known that when I should be caught, he would give me a thousand lashes.

The woman went and fetched me about two ounces of bread, of which I ate a small portion—wishing to keep the rest to eat in the swamp,—husbanding it, as much as possible. When she told me that I should receive a thousand lashes, I felt horrified and wept bitterly. The girl wept also. I had seen a slave who had escaped to the Northern States, and, after an absence of four years, had been brought back again and flogged, in the presence of all the slaves assembled from the neighbouring plantations. His body was frightfully lacerated. I went to see him two or three weeks after the flogging. When they were anointing his back, his screams were awful. He died soon afterwards—a tall, fine young fellow, six feet high, in the prime of life, thus brutally murdered.

All this flashed across my mind when I heard from the girl the threat of the thousand lashes. "Oh, dear," I said, "shall I ever suffer one thousand lashes? Shall I ever get to free Canada?" I went on, repeating these sentences over and over again in the most distracted manner all the way to my place of retreat.

Driven in a day or two after this to seek some food, I ventured across the country again, about two or three miles, when I came to a log-house. I approached slowly, looking anxiously around lest any one should be about. It was a fine moonlight night, and, I think, a little after twelve o'clock. I listened, and not hearing any one stirring, I looked through the window and saw a white man and woman in bed. At first I thought I would make my wants known to them; and then—remembering that white people had given up slaves and had received rewards, and had threatened if the slaves attempted to run away to shoot them—I hesitated, and, looking around, I saw a piece of wood with which I gently raised the window. I first cautiously put one leg in; and then, listening, I heard them snoring. I drew my other leg in, and passed the bed gently, and went into what from the pots and pans about I guessed was the kitchen. I looked and felt about for something to eat; not finding anything, I was coming out when my elbow knocked against a cupboard-door. I felt in, and found a ham-bone with about an ounce of meat on it. I hastened out of the window as quickly as possible, and closed it. I soon picked every morsel from the bone. In my cavern I sucked the bone until I went to sleep, and when I awoke in the morning I sucked it again, until it was completely polished. Whenever I now see a dog picking a bone, I remember the luxury it was to me.

A few nights afterwards, driven by hunger, I ventured out again, and, about four miles from the swamp, I came up to where I saw a house. I noticed on the ground what I thought was a goose, and, going gently up, I caught hold of it, when instantly it barked, for it was a dog. Having been caught in its sleep, it was evidently frightened, and howled fearfully. I ran back towards the bush, but had not proceeded many yards before a shot whistled past me, and I heard the report of a gun. I was running in a stooping position, or I think the shot would have penetrated my head. I regained my hiding-place—faint, wearied and disheartened.

Driven almost to desperation, the next night I went again in search of food. I had wandered about for some hours, without finding anything, when I saw a number of stumps of trees, two or three feet high; and about a hundred and fifty yards away from them I noticed a log hut. I approached it by degrees, hiding first behind one stump and then another. I waited for a short time, looking round to spy out something to eat. I observed a white woman with an Indian basket[46] come out of the house and walk towards a brick oven at some distance from the house, which is

46. Generally referred to a basket woven from wood splints, sliced and flattened from oak or ash, and sometimes dyed and decorated with patterns associated with particular Indian tribes.

usual in that country; she opened the oven-door and took some loaves out until she had filled her basket, and then taking it in her arms she carried it into the house. As soon as she had entered the house I ran to the oven, hoping to pick up a few crumbs, when to my utter surprise I found a loaf (surely the Lord had so ordained it); I hastily bit two or three pieces from it, and ran back to a stump. The woman came out of the house again, this time without the basket, and went to the oven, looked into it, and then, as if the devil himself were after her, she ran as I never saw a woman run before or since to the house.

I made all the haste I could to the cavern in the swamp. Oh! what a luxury that loaf was! I was afraid to let the mouthfuls go down my throat, it was so pleasant to taste the bread, and I was afraid it would soon be all gone. Never shall I forget that heaven-sent loaf and the prayers of gratitude I offered up to the Giver of all good things for it.

Driven by Hunger, give myself up to my Master.

My loaf was soon gone, and I was in the same state of hunger and desperation as before, when driven almost to my wits' end, and seeing no possible mode of escape (not being able to swim, I could not cross the Ohio River), I resolved to go to a Methodist preacher of the name of Brush, whom I knew, and entreat him to intercede with my master for me. I went towards his house, hesitating and pausing every now and then, hoping something would suggest itself to my mind even now by which I might escape. At length I knocked at the door. He came and looked at me. I spoke a few words to him, when he asked me who I was. I told him; he said he only knew me by my voice. His wife came to me and wanted to give me some food, for she seemed shocked at my appearance. Her husband insisted that she should not, since, he said, I was hungred [*sic*], and the food would perhaps kill me, and he should be blamed. However, she gave me one cup of tea and a slice of bread. Mr. Brush had promised to ask forgiveness for me, but he did not speak kindly to me. He put his hat on to go, and I followed him across the street, when a crowd of thoughts rushed across my mind,—the 1,000 lashes, the poor man whom I had seen flogged to death, the threats the woman ploughing in the fields had told me my master had made. I felt my strength gone; I stood, my brain swimming round. I thought I should fall, when Mr. Brush, turning suddenly round, in a sharp tone said, "Come on! Come on! Quick!" I followed him; we had ten or twelve miles to walk; he said but very little, and that not kindly, all the way. He seemed sullen. He said I should not have run away. At length, wearied and ready to drop, we got to my master's house. Mr. Brush entered, and I heard him say, "I have brought your slave Francis."[47] My master exclaimed, "What! you have! Well, I will do for him." I heard his footsteps, he came and looked at me, but said nothing. My mistress came, and said, "Francis! is that you?" I said, "Yes, missis, I have been longing to see you." "Come in," she said, "you are very bad for running away; now you must promise me only to eat just what I shall give you." I was weak, and sat down in the kitchen. A black woman was doing my work. Small portions of food were given me at a time each day. A little tea and dry toast, then a little milk, then a little bread and butter. I remained in the kitchen assisting, as my strength returned, the black woman. In about three weeks I found my former strength returning. During the three weeks, I had from time to time begged of my mistress not to have me whipped. She said she would do all she could if I would be a good slave in future. She spoke and treated me kindly.

Receive 107 Lashes.

At the end of about a month my master, one morning, came into the kitchen; he had a rope and a cow-hide whip in his hands. "Francis!" he said. "Yers, massa," I answered. "Come this way, I will now settle with you; you have been away nine weeks, and I will now reckon with you." I dropped on my knees, and begged hard for mercy. But all in vain. He produced a revolver and said, "Look here, if you attempt to run away, I will shoot you as sure as you are alive. Strip instantly." I took my clothes

47. This account of the Reverend Brush's intervention and attitude differs slightly from that given in the 1859 narrative, where the actions and words of the minister are described more neutrally, and he could be seen to be more sympathetic to Fedric's plight.

off, and he fastened me to an apple-tree behind the house, and flogged me until he was tired. I could not cry any more. The slaves who were watching me told me afterwards that I had received 107 lashes. He untied me; I could scarcely walk. For one cent, he swore, he would shoot me. He threatened, if ever I attempted to do so again he would certainly do for me. I crawled into the kitchen. I thought I should die. After dinner was over in the parlour, the servants looked at my back, which was frightfully lacerated, and rubbed it with something. Generally before this, after I had had a whipping, my master had ordered my back to be attended to, and salt to be applied, but this time he did not seem to care whether I recovered or not. In the evening my mistress came into the kitchen, and said, "Francis, you have had a very severe flogging. I could not prevent it. I hope you will never attempt to run away again. I thought your master would have killed you (she had been watching the flogging from a window); you must not be sullen or sulky to him in any way, or he will flog you again. I shall send you something into the kitchen to rub your back with," and after some more advice and cautions she went away.

Brutally Treated by my Master.

Slowly I began to recover; but now, after about fourteen years, I feel the effects of it, especially in bad weather.[48] I was dreadfully frightened of my master ever after this flogging. Whenever he had been whipping any of the slaves in the fields, and came into the kitchen, he would cut at me, or when drunk would make me stand with my hands down, and strike me in the face and ribs, and threaten, if I got out of his way, to shoot me with his revolver, which he always carried with him. "Blast the lot of them," he used to say; "when I begin, if I had strength, I would flog the whole plantation round." When he had been in the fields flogging the slaves for anything or nothing, and was returning home, he would stop to scratch his pet pig, which would stretch itself out, evidently enjoying life. He would call it master's pig, master's pig. He would then pat his favour-

48. Assuming this narrative was dictated in 1863, the year of its publication, the whipping Francis has just described would have taken place in 1849.

ite dog, which had run to meet him and was gambolling about him, calling it master's dog, master's dog. Then coming into the kitchen he would
make a dash at me, striking and lashing me several times, not caring
whether he hit me on the head or elsewhere. The girl would rush out of
the kitchen, but calling her back, he would curse her, and ask her "what
the h——— she was screaming for," and threaten to give her a whipping.
After having lashed her two or three times he would then pass upstairs.
Oh, how often have I looked at that pig and dog and wished I was either
rather than a black man!

CHAPTER VIII.

Produce of Kentucky—Climate of Kentucky—How the Kentuckians
Spend the Winter—Fevers Rage in Summer—Slaveholders frequently
administer Medicine to Slaves—Anecdote—The Domestic Animals—
The Birds—Change of Property, how it affects the
Slaves—Resignation of a Female Slave.

I still had to work on, now hopeless of ever getting my liberty. I was now very busy in the kitchen preserving various kinds of fruits. The fruit trees are generally in bloom in March. There are large orchards containing apple, peach, plum, pear, and damson trees, also gooseberries, currants, and raspberries. What we termed the sweet grape grows abundantly in the gardens; in the bush a vine grows wild bearing a very large grape, but it is sour. There are also great quantities of mulberries grown. There is a very nice fruit in the bush called the black and red haugh.[49] In the beginning of June there are plenty of ripe apples, indeed, there are apples of different kinds becoming ripe until December; large quantities of them are preserved. The apples are peeled and cut from the core, then stewed down in a pan containing cider, and put into jars; this is called apple butter, and is very nice and sweet to put upon bread in the winter time. There are enormous quantities of preserved fruits of all kinds put away in jars in the cellars. The slaves gather the apples and peaches when ripe, and take them to the distillery, and there beat them up in large troughs. This is put into tubs and ferments. Apple brandy, which is very strong, is made from it. Peach brandy, made in a similar manner, is mild. The spouse (pulp) is thrown out into the distillery-yard for the pigs; hence there are drunken

49. I.e., "haw." Fedric is referring to a species of hawthorne tree, also called the mayhaw, with fruit like the crabapple, which grows in the southern states. It is still used to make jam and jelly.

pigs as well as teetotal pigs. The pigs, after eating some spouse, will get up and grunt, grunt, grunt, and then down they will fall, to the infinite delight of the children. Some of the pigs, after being drunk two or three times, will not touch the spouse afterwards, thus teaching a very good lesson to us.

The principal produce of Kentucky is flax, hemp, tobacco, and excellent crops of wheat, except when the weevil and other insects, owing to the shortness of the winter and want of frost, destroy, in some measure, the crops. Large tracts of land are cultivated with Indian corn, which is the chief article of food for the negroes, and it is cooked for the use of the planters in a variety of ways, and is very much liked by strangers at the tables of the planters. I myself can cook it in ten different ways. Lately, prior to the war, the slaveholders of Kentucky had large patches of cotton. I must not forget to mention the excellent crops of sweet potatoes. Many of the slaves are allowed to keep the small potatoes for seed; and as the white people do not save the seed, the negroes sell them in the spring, and thus have a little money with which to purchase a few things for themselves. There is a very pleasant drink made from cherries, called cherry bounce, by mixing two-thirds of the juice with one-third of whiskey. Although such great quantities of fruit are grown, the slaves dare not, generally, touch any except it is given to them, which is very seldom, the Almighty not having sent the fruits of the earth for the slaves, but for their masters.

Climate of Kentucky.

The weather in Kentucky is very hot from the beginning of June to the middle of October. Europeans at first with difficulty can bear the heat in July and August. The cause of the intense heat is the absence of rain for some time. The heat from the sun in these months is very often such that it dazzles the eyes so that persons can only see distinctly at short distances. I remember at two large Camp Meetings in Fleming County,[50]

50. Fleming County lies next to Mason County on its southern border, and would be quite close to the area where the Parker plantation was.

water was sold at four pence per cup. The heat having dried up all the streams around, the water had to be brought three or four miles. The winters generally commence a little after Christmas, the cold, sharp winds beginning then to blow. It freezes for a day or two, when the ground becomes as hard as a brick, and then a thaw sets in, and in a day or two more it freezes again. The winters vary very much; one winter the ice will come floating down the river Ohio, in large pieces, the next winter perhaps the Ohio will be frozen so hard that hundreds of teams are crossing and recrossing it in all directions.[51] The ice generally breaks up about the end of February.

How the Kentuckians Spend the Winter.

From Christmas to March the planters keep up a perpetual succession of evening parties; there is nothing but fiddling and dancing, and "ladies-chain,"[52] and "cross half over." Many ladies dance so long that often they are carried in a fainting state out of the room. Balls and visiting continue the whole winter through; they seem to live for nothing else. The weather is so changeable that often when parties have gone over the snow on a sledge, the next day there is not a vestige of ice or snow left, and they are compelled to return on wheels. Generally winter is the easiest time for the slaves, who if they can get out for a dance do so, at least as many as are inclined. The slaves in Kentucky are better clothed and fed, far better, than in Virginia.

Fevers Rage in Summer.

Fevers are very prevalent in Kentucky, many of the planters losing during the summer months large numbers of slaves. I have seen the planters, who have lost their slaves by fever, walking about with clenched

51. The freezing over of the Ohio allowed some slaves to escape across the river on foot. Harriet Beecher Stowe's account in *Uncle Tom's Cabin* of Eliza fleeing across the ice to freedom is based on actual incidents, and especially the story of Eliza Harris, who escaped with her child, jumping from ice floe to ice floe, in 1838.

52. A square dance.

fists distracted, and saying, "I shall have to take the money I put away to buy more slaves," and almost cursing the Almighty for depriving them of their property. My master was one of this stamp.

Slaveholders Frequently Administer Medicine to Slaves.

The planters are in the habit of giving all their slaves medicine at the commencement of spring, that it may go easier with them in case of fever. In fact, they constantly resort to medicine in case of the slightest indisposition.

Anecdote.

I had a cousin who was fond of drink. One night he went to a distillery, where a black man was distilling, and got some whiskey, which made him drunk. Next morning he was crying, "Oh! oh! oh! me can't work to-day. Jee-e-ry," he said, "can't you go to de house and tell Massa I's sick to-day? I's so sick, me couldn't live to get out into de fields if me was to start." Jerry went to the house and told my master that Reuben was very sick. My master took some calomel[53] with him, and went to the cabin. "Well, Reuben," he said, "are you sick to-day?" Reuben putting his hand to the side of his head, said, "Yes, Massa, I's very sick indeed, Massa." "Where is the pain?" said my master. "All over me, in my head and back, all over me, Sir," said Reuben. "What time did your illness commence?" said my master. "Me tinks, as well as me can bemember, two clock dis morning," answered Reuben. "I have got something which will suit all your complaints,—calomel and jalap,"[54] said my master. Reuben's eyes flew wide open, "Massa, Massa," he said, "don't you tink if me was to walk bout in de air it might help me widout takin dat?" "No, no," said my master, "I want you to take this and stay in to-day, and if you feel better you can go out to-morrow." He ordered Aunty, who

53. A heavy, soft, white, sweetish-tasting mineral, also called mercurous chloride, that has been used as a purgative since the sixteenth century.

54. Jalap is another unpleasant-tasting purgative made from the roots of the jalap (Ipomea purga) bindweed.

takes care of the children, to give him some blood-warm water in a cup. "Now, Reuben," he said, "you drink this physic down, and then take a little water after it, and rinse your mouth with some more." Reuben swallowed the physic, and pulled such a face as I never saw in all my life. My master left the cabin saying, "Now, if you feel better you can go out tomorrow." Reuben got drunk again, another night about three months afterwards. Next morning he was hollering[55] out, "Oh! oh! oh! me know me die afore night, me does feel so bad." "Reuben," said Jerry. "Wh-a-at deyah want?" answered Reuben. "Can me go to de house and tell Massa dat you sick gen?" replied Jerry. "No, no, M-Massa, -M-Massa will come down 'ere an bring some more of dat calomer and jolloper," stammered out Reuben.

But to return from this little digression to my account of the produce of Kentucky.

The Domestic Animals.

They pride themselves very much on the breed of their horses, mules, bullocks, sheep, and pigs. The winter destroys a great many sheep, because they are housed without sufficient ventilation. They are compelled to house the sheep on account of the great number of wolves roaming about in winter.

The Kentuckians do not in general begin to break in their horses until they are four or five years old; consequently many accidents happen to the riders, their horses being often very restive.

The houses of the planters are built of brick and stone, and generally a verandah runs right round them; the kitchens are situated at a short distance from the house, so that the cooking may not be smelt.

The Birds.

The woods are full of birds, with plumage of almost every colour, black, blue, green, &c.—the mocking bird, whip-poor-will, and many

55. Original version has "holloing."

others whose names I do not know, and birds with most melodious notes. There is a large bird called the turkey buzzard, which lives upon dead animals. It is wonderful to see them perched in the trees by hundreds when a dead animal is near. They watch until the bald-eagle comes and takes the eyes out of the carcass, apparently being afraid as long as the eyes are there; but they are no sooner out than down the buzzards fly and swarm about it, picking every morsel of flesh from the bones. The quill of the buzzard is valued to make pens of, being much better than the goose quill. They are a very harmless bird, and not easily frightened by the presence of man, since he rarely disturbs them, on account of their being such excellent scavengers to clear the ground of dead animal matter. There is a fowl living in the water as large as a wild duck, called the water witch,[56] which is as black as jet. It can be approached within a yard, and any one would suppose that, being so near, he could easily strike it. But in a twinkling, when aimed at, it darts down, appears again at some distance, and will allow you to approach near again, seemingly thinking that it can avoid the intended blow. Although I have struck at many, and seen others strike, I never once saw one hit. Hence, I should suppose its name. There are the woodcock and woodpecker, and a variety of squirrels, some of them, especially the fox-squirrel, being very large, which destroy great quantities of corn.

In short, Kentucky is a very beautiful country; and, as I heard a gentleman remark, "All but the spirit of man is divine."

Change of Property.—How it affects the Slaves.

And so, my reader, you would think if I could bring before your mind's eye the lovely landscape, and then open out to you the interior of that fine house, with a splendid lawn in the front, looking upon as magnificent scenery as you perhaps ever saw. I will tell you something about its owner. His name is O—— B——,[57] the nephew of a kindhearted

56. A popular name for the pied-billed grebe, a small ducklike bird found in rivers and lakes.

57. Oscar Bower. Amy Parker, mother of Richard and William Parker, who also

planter, Mr. P——, recently dead, and who had left a fine tobacco plantation and 150 slaves to Mr. B——, of Virginia, a slave-breeding State. Being a house-slave myself, I became acquainted with the housemaids, waiting-maids, and other slaves about Mr. P——'s house. And I am sure I never saw more modest and better-behaved girls in my life than they were. Perfect models of propriety. Their neatness, good conduct, and virtuous conversation were praised by all. Mr. P—— left this property in Kentucky to his sister's eldest son, the present proprietor.

But, oh, what a sad change! My heart is full when I recall to mind the forced pollution of one after another of these good girls. Satiated with one, he would force another to submit to his lusts, in spite of all their entreaties. Soul and body they were bound to him. Louisa was the first who was taken, and in secret, among her friends, the sorrowful conversation about her degradation I well remember. Aunt Celia, poor Louisa's mother, went one day to the house to ask that her daughter might spend a night at her cabin. "Come in, come this way," said Mr. B——, quite mildly. Aunt Celia followed him. He took her into a spinning-room, tied her to a loom, tore the clothes from her back and said, "How dare you insult me by asking such a thing?" and flogged her within an inch of her life, her wretched son and daughter, who heard her shrieks for mercy, not daring to intercede. Imagine the feelings and thoughts of the unhappy girl spending that night by the side of her mother's torturer and her tyrant polluter.

Surely ungoverned lust makes man a fiend. Poor Jane made an attempt to resist, but he presented a loaded revolver at her head, and threatened to send all its contents into her. She shared the same fate as Louisa. Two or three more were served in a similar manner. But why need I dwell upon the sickening details. Good reader, you can imagine them; and the worst you can imagine will not be a tenth part so bad as the reality. Such is the ever-impending fate of the slave. To-day kindly treated, virtuous,

moved from Virginia to Kentucky with her sons in the first decades of the nineteenth century, bequeathed her slaves to her grandson, Oscar Bower. The inventory of William Parker, dated 1830, includes Cecilia and Louisa among the slaves (Mason County Courthouse Records, Will Book H, 115).

timorous of the future, yet comparatively happy. A death, a debt, or any change of property, plunges them, in spite of themselves, into unspeakable horrors, brutality, shame, and woe. Surely the Lord of all will soon blot out such things from the face of His fair creation.

Resignation of a Female Slave.

I can scarcely convey by any description the spirit of complete resignation and hope for the future manifested by religious slaves when suffering as no one but slaves could suffer. The following anecdote will illustrate what I mean. My master had a slave, by name Milly, who used to sing when she was milking the cow (for Milly was constantly singing psalms and hymns); when she stopped singing, the cow gave no milk, but as soon as the cow heard the song again, she gave her milk. My mistress has often taken visitors to see this. Poor Milly was one day being flogged for some trifling fault, and my master threatening to kill her because she did not say what slaves being whipped generally do cry out, "Oh, pray massa; oh, pray massa," she looked round at him so innocently and pitifully, and said, "De sooner you kill me de sooner me go home to Jesus; He be better massa dan you." At last he did not whip her for any little error, and the slaves said he was afraid of killing her, lest she should be happy.

CHAPTER IX.

*Cruelty to Slaves Concealed from Strangers—Slaveholders traduce
the English—Slaves' Opinions of the English—Slaves
always anxious to be Free.*

Travellers and strangers passing through the Southern States have no conception of the cruelty practised around them; it is kept in the background. My master was ordering two slaves to strip, for the purpose of flogging them for having been out without leave during the night. Two gentlemen rode up to the house, and called to my master, and asked him in a nasal tone if he had 1,000 cattle for sale, a boasting way characteristic of the Yankees. My master, perceiving instantly that they were Northerners, said to the two slaves, "Put your things on quickly. Make haste, boys"; and, addressing the gentlemen, said, "I have got nine or ten"; and turning to the two slaves, "Now, my boys, fetch up the cattle for the gentlemen; be as quick as you possibly can, that's good fellows," speaking in the kindest and blandest tones possible. The cattle broke away and got into the field again; my master, not appearing in the least irritated, encouraged the two slaves, in a very kind way, to bring them up again, which, after some time, they succeeded in doing. The cattle were sold and driven northwards by some men belonging to the two gentlemen. Some slaves heard one of the gentlemen call to the drivers, and say, "Did you ever hear a northern gentleman speak more kindly to his men than that slave owner did to his slaves?" "Never, never in all our lives," the drivers replied. "Well, then," said the gentleman, "I will never, as long as I live, believe one word about the cruelty of the slave owners; it is all a foul libel; they are only a great deal too kind."

As soon as the two gentlemen who had purchased the cattle had departed, my master took the money which he had received and put it away in the house, and then called the two slaves to him and said, "Now, you scoundrels, come and have your rations." Each one was stript, and received a most cruel whipping, their backs being cut in the most horrible manner, the poor slaves calling and shrieking out for mercy, but calling in vain; their cries ascending to heaven at the very time when the two northern gentlemen were protesting that every word about the cruelty of the southern planter was false.

Opinions of Slaves concerning the English.

Is it to be wondered at that slaves are almost always, when they have a chance, talking privately about escaping, and getting away to Great Britain's land, as Canada is called? "You had better be a slave here than live in any of the British Islands," said a gentleman, a neighbour of my master, one day to his slave. "If you were in any of the British possessions, and were to speak against the Government, they would take you, put your head upon a block, and chop it off. It would then dance up and down apart from the body, which would be wriggling about." "Massa, is dat de way dey do?" said the slave, laughing. "Yes; and if you were to speak against the Queen, they would make a great fire and burn you alive." "Massa, is dat de way dey do?" said the slave, still laughing; "will Massa let me go see?" "No, go along to your work," answered the irritated master. The negroes, although kept in the grossest ignorance, cannot but be aware of the systematic means adopted to debase them, and, in spite of all the masters can do, the slaves see through their shallow pretended reasons for oppressing them. However sedulously the slaveholders may shut their slaves up from the outer world, and may distort anything and everything which is contrary to their interests, yet the power of truth is too great for them. Wonderfully subtle is the atmosphere of opinion, penetrating where it is least wanted. Every slave to a man has the most exalted idea of Great Britain and her possessions. Whenever we slaves have been together talking, we have always wished to be among the "Britainers." We looked upon them as something very much superior to Americans. There was a charm about the word British which I cannot convey to any one. It meant, associated as it was in our minds with the abolition of slavery, everything which was noble and good.[58] I never in my life knew a slave who did not wish to escape. Several I have known who were well-treated, and, if liberated, would willingly and gladly have remained with their masters, but the fear of the "trader" constantly made them uneasy.

58. Fedric notes, "I remember anxiously asking, when I escaped into Canada, to be shown a Britainer, and a fine portly specimen was pointed out to me, who, to my infinite delight, shook me by the hand, and congratulated me upon my escape."

CHAPTER X.

An Abolitionist Planter contrives my Escape—My Escape by the
"Underground Railway"—Land in Canada—Employed by the Anti-Slavery
Society—Marry—Arrive in England—Conclusion.

Since my first attempt to escape I was so uniformly treated badly, that my life would have been insupportable if I had not been soothed by the kind words of the good abolitionist planter who had first conveyed to me a true knowledge of religion.[59] I had been flogged, and went one day to show him the state in which I was. He asked me what I wanted him to do. I said, "To get me away to Canada." Oh, what a delightful word to us poor slaves! It was like speaking of some heavenly country. There was music in its sound to our ears. Never did tempest-tossed sailor long so much for a haven as we did for that land of the free. When I mentioned Canada to the gentleman, he sat for full twenty minutes thoughtfully, and at last said, "Now, if I promise to take you away out of all this, you must not mention a word to any one. Don't breathe a syllable to your mother or sisters, or it will be betrayed." Oh, how my heart jumped for joy at

59. There was considerable abolitionist sentiment in Kentucky, especially among workingmen and craftsmen, who, at a mass meeting in Louisville in 1849, declared slavery "injurious to both slaves and owners, degraded labour, and interfered with employment for free citizens" (Charles E. Hedrick, "Negro Slavery in Kentucky before 1850" [M.A. thesis, University of Chicago, 1915]). However, relatively few emancipists were as radical as the Reverend John Fee, who demanded instant abolition. The *Anti-Slavery Bugle* (February 16, 1849) reported that 523 emancipists in Mason County had signed a call for the emancipation convention that was held in Mason County on February 12, 1849. Resolutions were adopted calling for a "gradual and prospective system of emancipation accompanied by colonization." Although the issue of emancipation was central to the debate held at the Kentucky Constitutional Convention in May 1850, property rights of slave owners were declared sacrosanct (Asa Earl Martin, *The Anti-Slavery Movement in Kentucky, Prior to 1850* [Louisville: Standard Printing Company, 1918], 124–37).

this promise. I felt new life come into me. Visions of happiness flitted before my mind. And then I thought before the next day he might change his mind, and I was miserable again. I solemnly assured him I would say nothing to any one. "Come to me," he said, "on the Friday night about ten or eleven o'clock; I will wait till you come. Don't bring any clothes with you except those you have on. But bring any money you can get." I said I would obey him in every respect. I went home and passed an anxious day. I walked out to my poor old mother's hut, and saw her and my sisters. How I longed to tell them, and bid them farewell. I hesitated several times when I thought I should never see them more. I turned back again and again to look at my mother. I knew she would be flogged, old as she was, for my escaping. I could foresee how my master would stand over her with the lash to extort from her my hiding-place. I was her only son left. How she would suffer torture on my account, and be distressed that I had left her for ever until we should meet hereafter in heaven, I hoped.

At length I walked rapidly away, as if to leave my thoughts behind me, and arrived at my kind benefactor's house a little after eleven o'clock. He said but little, and seemed restless. He took some rugs and laid them at the bottom of the wagon, and covered me with some more. Soon we were on our way to Maysville, which was about twenty miles from his house. The horses trotted on rapidly, and I lay overjoyed at my chance of escape. When we stopped at Maysville, I remained for some time perfectly quiet, listening to every sound. At last I heard a gentleman's voice, saying, "Where is he? where is he?" and then he put in his hand and felt me. I started, but my benefactor told me it was all right, it was a friend. "This gentleman," he added, "will take care of you; you must go to his house." I got out of the wagon and shook my deliverer by the hand with a very, very grateful heart, you may be sure; for I knew the risk he had run on my account. He wished me every success, and committed me to his friend, whom I accompanied to his house, and was received with the utmost kindness by his wife, who asked me if I was a Christian man. I answered yes. She took me up into a garret and brought me some food. Her little daughters shook hands with me. She spoke of the curse of slavery to the land. "I am an abolitionist," she said, "although in a slaveholding country. The work of the Lord will not go on as long as slavery is carried on here." Every possible attention was paid to me to soothe my troubled mind. The following night the gentleman and his son left the house about ten o'clock, and had not returned at twelve. I was crying, being afraid they could not manage it. The lady assured me her husband would get a skiff, if even he had to break the lock (skiffs are chained and locked to the shore). However, a little after twelve o'clock the gentleman returned, and said he had got a boat and I was to go with him. His lady bid me fare-well, and told me to put my trust in the Lord, in whose hands my friends were, and asked me to remember them in my prayers, since they had hazarded everything for me, and, if discovered, they would be cruelly treated. I was soon rowed across the river, which is about a mile wide in that place.[60] The son remained with me in the skiff whilst his father went to a neighbouring village to bring some one to take charge of me. After some time, he brought a friend, who told me never to mention the name

60. True to his word, Fedric does not in any of his narratives reveal the names of those who helped him escape. Escapes by fugitive slaves across the Ohio by boat from Maysville to Ripley were not uncommon in the 1850s and earlier. An article in the *Louisville Courier* (December 14, 1855) reports "some ten or twelve slaves have within the last week made their escape from Maysville and its vicinity." John Parker, who had purchased his freedom, lived in Ripley and stated that he rowed on average one fugitive a week across the river (Hudson, *Fugitive Slaves*, 152). Arnold Gragston, himself a slave on a plantation near Maysville, declared that he took about one hundred fugitives across the river, making three or four trips a month. He worked with the Kentucky abolitionist minister John Fee. He describes how "it would have to be the 'black nights' of the moon when I would carry them, and I would meet them out in the open or in a house without a single light. The only way I knew who they were was to ask them, 'What you say?' And they would answer 'Menare.' I don't know what that word meant—it came from the Bible. I only know that was the password I used, and all of them I took over told it to me before I took them" (quoted in Keith P. Griffler, *Front Line of Freedom: African Americans and the Forging of the Underground Railroad in the Ohio Valley* [Lexington: University Press of Kentucky, 2004], 96). Fedric may have been lodged briefly in the house of John Rankin, pastor of the Presbyterian Church in Ripley from 1822 to 1866. One of his sons claimed that his family "lodged and forwarded not less than 2000 slaves" (Hudson, *Fugitive Slaves*, 153).

of any one who had helped me; and that when I got to Canada I might write and tell my master of my escape, but never to allude to those who had in any way assisted me, and to ask the blessing of the Lord for them. He took me to his house outside the town, where I had some refreshment, and remained about half-an-hour. A wagon came up, and I was stowed away, and driven about twenty miles that night, being well guarded by eight or ten young men with revolvers. It would do any real Christian man good to see the enthusiasm and determination of these young Abolitionists. Their whole heart and soul are in the work. A dozen such men would have defied a hundred slaveholders. From having seen over and over again slaves dragged back chained through their country, and having heard the tales of horrible treatment of the poor hopeless captives, some having been flogged to death, others burnt alive, with their heads downwards, over a slow fire, others covered with tar and set on fire,—these noble, courageous, self-sacrificing men have been so wrought upon that they are heroes of the highest stamp, and I verily believe they would willingly lay down their lives rather than allow one fugitive slave to be taken from them.

On I went, from one station to another, everywhere being received and lodged as if I were a chosen guest. If it was after midnight, all in the house, even to the old grandmother and little children, would get up and crowd round me, listening to my sorrows, and shedding alternately tears of joy and grief for my escape and the bitter pangs I had had to endure. How shall I, who, to the age of fifty, was a poor illiterate slave, find adequate language to express my eternal gratitude to them! He who is above, and is the Lord and Master of us all, I know will reward them for their goodness. To Him I pray as I pass the day,[61] and as I lie awake in the silent hours of the night, to pour blessings upon them.

I came at last to a large station of what is called the Underground Railway, about 160 miles from the banks of the Ohio river. But think not, you who read this, that my mind was at rest. Two or three nights in succession I dreamt that I was taken by my master, and all the details of the capture were so vividly depicted in my dreams, that I could scarcely, when

61. Original has "pass on in the day."

awake, believe it was all a vision of the night. I should have been pleased to have entered more fully into particulars concerning these journeys from station to station, but my Quaker friends tell me it would be very injudicious to do so, since one or two fugitive slaves, having described things too minutely, had put the slaveholders upon the right track, and the Underground Railway had been torn up, to the injury of my brethren in bondage, who might otherwise have escaped.

At this large station I remained over the winter, from November to the middle of May. I had now got pretty well assured of my safety, and had the range of a large house. There was a family of eleven or twelve children, some grown-up young men and women. The younger portion of the children soon became very much attached to me, following me from room to room, and asking me to learn to read. I told them I was fifty years of age, and too old. Oh, no, they said, I could learn, and they would soon teach me. One day little Johnny, a fine fellow about twelve years of age, and his sister Charlotte, about ten, stood by my side with a book with the A, B, C, in large letters. "Can you see that?" said Johnny, pointing at the first letter. "Yes," I replied. "Well, then," they rejoined, laughing, "you can learn, for you can see. Now, that is A." Pointing to the next, "That is B. Oh, I see you can know them," said Johnny; and I felt I could tell the difference. Regularly did they teach me, often laughing at my mistakes, but still delighted whenever I, stupid enough no doubt, made an effort. I soon found I had conquered the letters. My little master and mistress were as proud of this victory as if it had been some noble achievement. Yes, and so it was, for it opened the gates of ignorance, and displayed to me a new world, part of which I could make permanently my own. Day by day I said to my little instructors my spelling, first of one syllable, and then of two, dozens of times over. It would have tired the patience of man or woman, but my little teachers were never out of temper, but persevered until I finally could read the first chapter of John.

Bless all the children in the world! I should have remained in ignorance if I had not been taught by them. When I see them gambolling about in their sports, how delighted I am. Often and often have I stood among them in the Sunday-school, and when the teacher has said "Boys," I have straightened myself up, and thought I was one of them. Wherever I go, I find they feel the influence of this kindly disposition towards them. They hang about me, take me by the hand, and never am I so happy as when I am surrounded by them. I can truly say, reverently, in the words of my sacred Master, "Suffer little children to come unto me, for of such is the kingdom of heaven."

About the middle of May, I was sent to Sindusky city,[62] on the borders of Lake Erie. But I shall never forget the prayers offered up for my welfare by the master, and the pain it gave me to part from my dear young friends. They would have willingly kept me always, they said; but I knew, although there was not much danger, yet there was risk, and I longed to be on British soil. I heard my friends bargain with the captain of a steamer to take me across the lake. He said, "Have you only one? I wish you had a hundred. I would gladly take them over." A noble, generous-hearted man he was!

I was landed at some town in Michigan, but I forget the name of the town.[63] The mate took me to an Abolitionist's house, who said he would forward me on to Canada. From this town I went to another place in Pennsylvania, and from thence to a minister's house in York State, who said jocosely that he had the strongest fort, next to Gibraltar, in the world. He said for fifteen miles round they were all Abolitionists, and I was perfectly safe; that, although he was acting contrary to the Fugitive Slave Law, he did it with pleasure, since he believed that law to be contrary to the law of God, and he willingly trampled it under his feet; that he had had at least thirty fugitive slaves before me.

After a few months, the Abolitionist gentlemen held a Meeting, and I told them some of my sufferings in slavery. They prayed with me; and I remember an old Quaker lady, shaking me by the hand, and speaking

62. Sandusky in northern Ohio, on the shores of Lake Erie, near Cedar Point, frequently used as a point of departure for fugitive slaves escaping to Canada.

63. Fedric's account of his route from here is puzzling, since he would have had to go west from Sandusky to Michigan, and then east again to northwestern Pennsylvania and New York State near Buffalo, from where he crossed to Canada via Lake Ontario. It is more likely that he was taken to Michigan before traveling to Sandusky. Robin W. Winks records that "the steamer *Arrow*, moving between Sandusky and Detroit under its noted Captain J. W. Keith, transported a large number of fugitives" (*The Blacks in Canada: A History* [New Haven: Yale University Press, 1971], 245).

kindly, said, "Thee must not, when thee gets to Canada, say, 'I have done it 'cute;[64] I have been Smart.' Thee must remember that it is the Lord who has been thy friend. Ask Him to give thee a portion of His Spirit; and give Him the glory and honour." I was passed on to Louistown,[65] on Lake Ontario, to be sent across to Toronto.

Land in Canada.

On Lake Ontario—unlike when I was on Lake Erie—although it was rough, I was not sick or ill; for my mind seemed so much on the stretch, and so elated with the thought that Canada was at hand, I felt nerved for anything, and could almost bound out of the steamer.

I gazed upon the people on shore, until I thought they would think I was wild; and, at last—thank the Lord for ever!—placed my foot on free British soil, in Toronto.[66]

But now, when I was in Toronto, under the British flag and the British rule, I found there was still the Yankee prejudice existing against my race, and a distinction and badge of inferiority, still clinging to me. Going into a barber's shop one day to be shaved, the master said, "What do you

64. A dialect word, a shortened form of "acute," meaning clever or smart.

65. Lewiston, which is situated close to Niagara Falls on the New York side.

66. Despite rebellions in upper and lower Canada in 1837, and the granting of "responsible government" by a Canadian legislature for domestic concerns, the province of Canada remained under British imperial rule until 1867. Slavery had been officially abolished in Canada (as in other British colonies) in 1833. However, as early as 1793, the governor of upper Canada (which included Ontario) had negotiated a bill that forbade the importation of slaves into the province and legislated for the freedom of the children of all existing slaves at the age of twenty-five. In 1829 a group of black people from Cincinnati, Ohio, petitioned to be allowed to settle in Canada under the protection of the British flag, and assurance of protection was given by the lieutenant governor, John Colbourne. According to Ian Pemberton, "over 11000 Cincinnati Negroes formed the first sizeable Negro community ever established on Canadian soil, the Wilberforce settlement, just north of London (Ontario)" (Ian Pemberton, "The Anti-Slavery Society of Canada" [M.A. thesis, University of Toronto, 1967], 10). See also C. Peter Ripley, ed., *The Black Abolitionist Papers, Vol. II: Canada, 1830–1865* (Chapel Hill: University of North Carolina Press, 1987). Winks estimates that by 1860 there were approximately 40,000 blacks in upper Canada, of which 30,000 were fugitive slaves (*The Blacks in Canada*, 240–41).

want?" I replied, "To be shaved." "Oh, we don't shave black men here," he said. I went towards the door, when, following me, the barber said, "If I were to shave you, I should lose all my customers; but you will find a shop down the street where they shave black men exclusively." Now, when I came to Liverpool and went into a shop to be shaved, when it came to my turn, I declined, saying the other gentlemen, who had come in after me, had better be shaved first; but after three or four more had been operated upon, they insisted that I should take the next turn. No one can possibly understand my delight and mingled feelings of pleasure and gratitude that I was, at last, placed on an equality with the white man; and, rising up, I could not refrain from ejaculating, loudly and sincerely, "God save the Queen!" to the astonishment and merriment of those in the place. Aye, true liberty is surely a pearl of great price. I felt, at last, completely disenthralled in mind and body.

Employed by the Anti-Slavery Society.[67]

But, to return to Toronto, I was soon employed by the Anti-Slavery Society there to look after the fugitive slaves. And I can assure my readers that this was to me, who could truly sympathize with them, a most heart-rending occupation. Haggard and emaciated, from anxiety and want of rest, men and women presented a most deplorable picture. Some of them were mulattoes and quadroons, and, being employed generally in household duties, they were very intelligent, and, in many cases, except to a

67. The Anti-Slavery Society of Canada was founded in 1851 in response to the Fugitive Slave Law and an influx of escaped slaves who could no longer find refuge in the northern states of America. On February 26, 1851, a public meeting at Toronto's city hall organized a society "to aid in the extinction of Slavery all over the world." Founded by local white clergymen and businessmen, and strongly supported by the *Toronto Globe*'s editor, George Brown, the society included several black people on its executive board. Among the most prominent were two fugitives, who also wrote their stories and became well-known speakers in Canada and the United Kingdom: Henry Bibb (who had also escaped from Kentucky) and Samuel Ringgold Ward. During its first year, the society focused its activities on aiding fugitive slaves, up to five thousand of whom crossed the Canadian border between 1850 and 1852, most without money or anything more than the clothing they wore (Ripley, *Black Abolitionist Papers, Vol. II*, 30; Pemberton, "The Anti-Slavery Society of Canada," 37).

practised eye, they could scarcely be distinguished from the pure white. Others were of coal-black colour, and, having been degraded to the uttermost by abuse and hardship on the plantations, seemed but little removed from an animal; but a short period of kindness and attention, and freedom, seemed to work wonders in the development of their minds.

Marry.

I soon found that at least in the minds of the English, there was not such a repugnance to, and prejudice against, my race; for I formed an attachment—I suppose at my age I must not call it love—to a Devonshire female, who was residing in Toronto, and I have the best of all reasons to suppose it was reciprocated, for I was accepted by her, and married her; and it was owing to her wishing to come among her friends, that has brought me to this grand old land of liberty.[68]

Arrive in England.

Armed with recommendations from the Rev. J. S. Ellerby,[69] minister of the First Congregational Church, Toronto, to the Rev. Dr. Raffles, of

68. I have not been able to locate with certainty a record of Fedric's marriage in Toronto and the name of his wife. A possible record is a marriage notice in the *Toronto Christian Guardian* (April 30, 1856, 3) for "Mr. Francis Frederick and Jane Flynn, both of Toronto, on April 22, 1856." (Francis Frederick is the name Fedric used after his return to the United States in 1865.) The Reverend James Borland, minister for the Wesleyan Methodist Church on Elm Street, officiated. Neither the address nor the nature of the minister, described in his obituary as a "champion of the oppressed, a man who felt righteous indignation at all kinds of tyranny" (*Christian Guardian*, May 16, 1888, 314), would conflict with the possibility that this particular marriage record might refer to the author of this narrative.

In his analysis of the 1861 census in Canada, Barry Noonan notes that the majority of black Canadians were members of the Wesleyan Methodist Church, and also that a significant number of black men married white women from England and Ireland. In St. John's Ward in Toronto (which included the Elm Street Methodist church), 12 out of the 107 families included mixed-race couples (Barry Christopher Noonan, *Blacks in Canada, 1861* [Madison, Wisc.: B. Noonan, 2000], 418–20).

69. Actually the Reverend T. S. Ellerby, appointed in 1855 as pastor of the First Congregational Church on Bay and Adelaide streets, Toronto, after serving as a minister in

Liverpool,[70] I bid farewell to that land of many sorrows, and, in the last few months, some joys and regrets to part from my kind benefactors.

I was kindly received, on my presenting my credentials, by that gentleman. Since then, to the best of my humble ability, and as much as my enfeebled health would permit, I have been engaged in various parts of the country, speaking concerning my own experience and escape from slavery, and lecturing, as well as I could, about slavery generally; thus doing my best for many who are still enduring what a merciful Providence has rescued me from.[71]

Conclusion.

I am not competent to enter into learned arguments about the natural rights of man, and the consequent wrongs inflicted by slavery on the African race. I have but little acquaintance with literature; but there is one Book, which I read as much as I can, and what it says I believe, and all the arguments of all the learned in the world are nothing to me, if they are opposed to what it says and teaches.

Bexley Heath, London. He is listed as a member of the Committee of the Anti-Slavery Society of Canada in its report for the years 1855–57.

70. Rev. Dr. Thomas Raffles (1788–1863), cousin of Stamford Raffles of Singapore, was minister of Great George Street Chapel in Liverpool for fifty years, and one of the most influential nonconformist ministers in the country at that time. In 1864, at a cost of 5,000 pounds, a large building comprising a workmen's hall, reading rooms, and a ragged school was erected on Greenland Street as a memorial to him.

71. A number of speakers were sent to the United Kingdom to help raise funds for the Anti-Slavery Society of Canada. They included the Reverend Samuel Ringgold Ward, who toured and lectured in England, Scotland, and Ireland. Ward was received in April 1853 by the Earl of Shaftesbury, and by the summer of 1854 had collected 1,200 pounds for the society (Pemberton, "The Anti-Slavery Society of Canada," 56). In his 1869 *Autobiography*, Francis Frederick, as he now inscribed himself, lists some of the places he visited, including Manchester, Birmingham, Worcester, Bristol, Plymouth, London, York, Newcastle, Glasgow, Edinburgh, Dundee, Aberdeen, Swansea, Dublin, and Belfast. The 1861 Scottish census locates him on April 6 in Stirling, Scotland, where his occupation is described as a lecturer. During the previous two weeks, reports of his lectures appeared in the *Dundee Advertiser* (see Introduction).

I was reading the other day the eighth chapter of the Acts of the Apostles, and I found a passage there so interesting to me, that I cannot refrain from transcribing it,[72] and asking you, candid reader, to see whether Philip—who is a greater authority, I have no doubt, with you, than all the slaveholders and their clerical supporters put together—objected to the Ethiopian, that his skin was black, and that he was of the African race?

No. No such things were suggested. The one thing required by Philip was belief in the Lord Jesus Christ; and, in order to induce that belief, the Apostle himself preached, that is, explained, to the Ethiopian, the wondrous prophecy concerning our Lord contained in the fifty-third chapter of the Prophet Isaiah.

Thus, I find, long before the Gospel was known to the ancestors of the slaveholders, the Lord had sent His heavenly messenger, with the glad tidings to my countrymen in Africa. There can be no true controversy about this. It is so plain that he that runs may read;[73] and, although my race may, by an inscrutable Providence, have been permitted to be oppressed for generations, yet, as they were among the first to receive His Spirit, I believe there is a good time at hand, when a fresh outpouring of it will be felt amongst them; the barriers being now breaking down, amidst the horrors of civil war.

Depend upon it, when the Gospel shall be preached to them, in its purity, the negro race will receive it, in its simplicity, and will show a higher Christian capacity than the world has given them credit for. The Gospel is just suited to their simple, forgiving, humane nature. May God hasten that time! is my sincere prayer.

72. Fedric is referring to the passage from the Acts of the Apostles which he has appended at the end of his narrative.

73. A popular misquotation of a biblical verse. The quotation from Hab. 2:2 is, "Write the vision, and make it plain, that he may run that readeth it." The saying may also have been adapted from William Cowper's "Tirocinium":

> But truths, on which depends our main concern . . .
> Shine by the side of every path we tread
> With such a lustre, he that runs may read.

And the angel of the Lord spake unto Philip, saying, Arise, and go toward the south unto the way that goeth down from Jerusalem unto Gaza, which is desert. And he arose and went: and, behold, a man of Ethiopia, an eunuch of great authority under Candace queen of the Ethiopians, who had the charge of all her treasure, and had come to Jerusalem for to worship, was returning, and sitting in his chariot read Esaias the prophet. Then the Spirit said unto Philip, Go near, and join thyself to this chariot. And Philip ran thither to him, and heard him read the prophet Esaias, and said, Understandest thou what thou readest? And he said, How can I, except some man should guide me? And he desired Philip that he would come up and sit with him. The place of the scripture which he read was this, He was led as a sheep to the slaughter; and like a lamb dumb before his shearer, so opened he not his mouth: in his humiliation his judgment was taken away: and who shall declare his generation? for his life is taken from the earth. And the eunuch answered Philip, and said, I pray thee, of whom speaketh the prophet this? of himself, or of some other man? Then Philip opened his mouth, and began at the same scripture, and preached unto him Jesus. And as they went on their way, they came unto a certain water: and the eunuch said, See, here is water; what doth hinder me to be baptized? And Philip said, If thou believest with all thine heart, thou mayest. And he answered and said, I believe that Jesus Christ is the Son of God. And he commanded the chariot to stand still: and they went down both into the water, both Philip and the eunuch; and he baptized him. And when they were come up out of the water, the Spirit of the Lord caught away Philip, that the eunuch saw him no more: and he went on his way rejoicing. But Philip was found at Azotus: and passing through he preached in all the cities, till he came to Cesarea.

—Acts 8:26–40

APPENDIX

LIFE AND SUFFERINGS

OF

FRANCIS FEDRIC,

WHILE IN SLAVERY,

AN ESCAPED SLAVE AFTER 51 YEARS IN BONDAGE

A TRUE TALE, FOUNDED ON FACTS,

SHEWING THE

HORRORS OF THE SLAVE SYSTEM.

LIFE AND SUFFERINGS OF FRANCIS FEDRIC WHILE IN SLAVERY.

I was born in Old Virginia, in Forquair [Fauquier] County, within nine miles of Cedar Run. My father was a slave, and worked for a tyrant master of the name of Carter; my mother was also a slave, and worked for a tyrant master of the name of Parker. My mother had nine children, two boys and seven girls; I and my brother and sisters worked for the same master. My grandmother was brought from Africa to Maryland, and then taken into Old Virginia, where she was purchased by my master's father; she was taught to repeat the Prayers and Liturgy of the Protestant Church by her young mistress, but my grandmother could not read, and notwithstanding the pains the wicked white people took to promote the belief that coloured people had no soul, my dear grandmother was anxious to impart to me and her other grand-children the knowledge of religious things according to her ability. She had a true enjoyment of religion herself, and by her conduct manifested hers was a living faith; she would repeat all the Liturgy and Creeds of her church by heart, and was anxious I should also commit them to memory, which oft times I was willing to do, but cruelty and wickedness prevailed over everything else, and I felt perplexed to know what I ought to believe. My mother was employed as a field-hand, and consequently, had she been able and willing, could not do much for me in the way of instruction, and I believe, so hard worked as she was, she had little thought of spiritual things as affecting herself and children, and so far as her instruction was concerned, I should have been as ignorant as the beasts that perish, but I rejoice that for a period of ten years she also experienced the consolation of religion.

My history and experiences by this time of course were affected by the known wasteful character of the slave system wherever it prevails, wasteful of all cultivation of mind and manners—of the fertility of the soil and of human labour—of social properties and religious observances; and whatever good of any kind may be obtained is in spite of the blighting tendencies of the nefarious system.

The system of farm cultivation in Virginia, where we raise tobacco and wheat, and on an estate to the best of my knowledge about 80 acres, cultivated by about 100 slaves, is generally understood to be much milder in its character for the slaves than where sugar or cotton are the staple products; but even in Old Virginia, under these more favourable conditions, slaving was hideous. See the swarms of young negroes huddling together like swine in straw by night, feeding on Indian corn broth out of troughs, served up very stintingly, so as to induce such eager eating as hunger only would produce, with its consequential quarrels and disorders; the children of so many families in a gang (under the care of an old negress generally called "Auntey") without shoes or covering for the head, their feet often in great chaps, sore and bleeding, their woolly heads sun-burnt to a reddish earth-colour, presenting a sad spectacle of neglect and degradation. That creatures in such circumstances should ever become in any degree subjects of religious emotions is a marvel.

When I was about fourteen years of age, my master removed his whole establishment to Kentucky. One incident which took place on our party having to pass through a town called Winchester, is a fair illustration of the slave-owner's bearing towards his fellow- citizens, as well as over his so-called own people; I went with my mother and about 15 other negroes, men and women, into a dry store (draper's); the people were very busy making their purchases, when my master abruptly entered the store, cracking his cane over the heads of the people, saying, "What are you doing here? What are you doing?" and the major part of the slaves could not have made better use of this opportunity. The store-keeper and his assistants were more astonished by the unexpected irruption of physical force than the people who seized on their selected goods, and perhaps something more, and helter-skelter away who should get out of the store and the master's beating first, the negroes carrying away with them not less than from £20 to £30 worth of goods unpaid for. We arrived in Kentucky, Mason County. We soon settled down to the work of clearing land and cultivating hemp and tobacco principally.

In about two or three years I was taken from negro quarters to dwell in the house as a servant, which pleased me much, as did the pains my mistress took to teach me a better talk than I had yet attained, although I found it very wearisome to repeat so often "I will" and "Go tell the ladies;" (an Englishman would be surprised at the difficulty of my acquiring the pronunciation so as to please my mistress); so that for two or three years I had tolerable times for one in bondage, until the death of my old master, who, although a free liver, or in other words [one who] gave vent to every lust, and from the terrors of his conscience he had a hard death. Yet such was the state of religion among the white people that he had a eulogistic sermon preached. The slaves thought it very strange that such a sermon should be preached for their old master, who, although not a cruel man to his slaves, was notoriously wicked. But his son, who succeeded him in the estate, was not much better in his general character, soon gave up to drink, and became unceasingly cruel to his slaves. And now I began to feel I should have been better off if I had been a field-labourer instead of a house-servant; my master became very irritable, running frequently from the parlour to the kitchen to vent his wrath upon the slaves there, especially when he had sporting, gambling, and drinking parties; he would invariably strike with a formidable whip made of raw cow-hide twisted, which he carried in his hand continually. My sufferings were great, I lived in terror which was renewed by the sound of anyone approaching the kitchen, so that I very soon began to wish myself out of it. But before I had time to mature my thoughts, [that] no man could have a right to hold me as his property and to torment me into conformity, or to make enquiries respecting the course I should take, I was driven on the impulse of a moment. My master established a rule that none of his slaves were to leave home without his permission; if we asked, he would question us very closely as to where we would go, who we would go to see, and so on, which was very unpleasant, and then he would drily say "stay at home." So that night, after such an interview and negative reply, and I had taken my own way, [and] I had observed his candle was out, I was then determined to go to the meeting among slaves in a neighbouring plantation. The next morning after I went to the meeting I was called up to the tree behind the kitchen, where he was in the habit of tying up his victims and flogging them, and as I had had a whipping of forty lashes, and my back still sore, and before he had time to tie me up for going to the meeting, I ran away thinking I could run faster than he. He set his blood-hounds after me. As I was cook, to the hounds I was no stranger, so that by clapping my hands I set them on the cattle, and so escaped into the bush. He called for his horse, not to pursue me, but to ride about to the neighbours for them to keep a look out, and ferry keepers he warned them not to allow me to pass over the Ohio river. He also offered a reward of 500 dollars to any one who would deliver me up to him or put me in confinement. I hid myself in the bush, and then I began to think what course I had better pursue. I wondered the hounds had not been put on my track; I feared they might yet come after me, and if I went on any road some one might capture me. I knew of a very dismal place known by the name of the Bear Wallow, about eighteen miles distant; present safety by concealment was the only thought that occupied my mind. To the swamp I arrived, and to the Bear Wallow where I found a recess under a high overhanging rock, at the side or foot of an hill. The recess was four feet from the ground; the swamp in which this retreat lay might be about nine miles either way. This wilderness was generally scoured by a turn-out of the neighbouring farmers and their friends once a month to drive back the wolves into the sugar loaf mountains; the bears they used to shoot. To this inhospitable and dangerous wild I could turn alone as it was seldom intruded on by man, my thoughts intent only on present safety from my cruel pursuer. My mind had never been accustomed to contemplate on the wonderfully changed condition of our father Adam when from the dust he was made a living creature. I had enjoyed the abundance of a well provided kitchen under a tyrant, distinguished for his parsimony in feeding his field hands in the respect of food, groaning and in terror because of the continual torments inflicted by my almost ever-present tormentor. I thought little of food the first and second day, nor did I feel much disposed for sleep. I soon discovered that if the large animals which were addicted to prowl on the neighbouring farms were driven out of this solitude, there was a numerous company of living things to disturb my repose and terrify me: whip-poor-will, a bird of that name, kept up his doleful cry in the bushes and trees, and around all night long frogs of every species croaking, and reptiles innumerable joining in wild concert. But not by their varied notes and sounds was I disturbed, the blowing snake with many others did not care to conceal themselves from my sight, their tameness was frightful to me from the first night or two. I felt no way disposed to a reclining posture among such multitudinous company, but nature soon required this indulgence, and my neighbours were emboldened to still greater familiarities; one would run right across me from one side to the other, one would lie still leaving his tail or his head partially on me, another would lie right across me as if to enjoy the full benefits of the comfort my body might afford as a bed. Reader, how do you suppose I knew that if one of those rattlesnakes struck at me, without good medical aid, the wound would be fatal in a few hours! Now I found that whatever faith I had was called into exercise, and while I avoided any kind of motion as much as possible unless I should provoke an attack, and I feared to indulge in sleep afraid I should involuntarily remove and offend my companions, the thoughts within me were active, and trusting in God, I had a rich enjoyment of peace, so that many a time since, when trials and troubles have been my lot, I have remembered that bed of reptiles and found comfort to my mind, even as David found encouragement from his former merciful deliverances and help to go out against Goliah [*sic*]. Yes, even though nature was craving for food, and by her handmaid hunger was urging me to seek food day by day, although I was fearful to embrace the opportunity the rising sun afforded me to gather such berries as the wilderness offered, many sorts of which were poisonous, and some would be certain death, some would cause bad swellings about the mouth and throat, so that, although very hungry, I was afraid to eat some sorts that I had not before proved, and was brought to feel my entire dependence upon Almighty God, my Heavenly Father, and through faith trusted and rejoiced in the good Shepherd, so that I had some good season in that inhospitable swamp.

But still the opportunity did not occur of crossing the river Ohio, and I was very fearful of shewing myself to anyone on account of the reward of 500 dollars offered for me. My weakness increased; although preserved from eating any poisonous berries my stomach would no longer retain such sorts as had hitherto been my only food. I was now extremely hungry and to obtain some food it was now inevitable I must run some risk by going into the inhabited part of the country, so that in about three or four weeks I ventured out by moonlight and after travelling what appeared to me an awful distance I arrived at a log house, with a nice patch of cultivated ground around it. I cautiously looked in at the window, the moon shone very brightly, and I saw a young couple fast asleep. I went round the house repeatedly but could see no other way into the house but through this same window, so I carefully entered and passed through their sleeping room. I searched their inner apartments and could find nothing but a bone left from a ham, which I took, and passed very quietly through the room where the happy couple still lay fast asleep, and returned to my hiding place. It was but a bare, a very bare bone, its saltness was very acceptable, and not only on my journey homeward, but several times during the night I awoke to suck and gnaw my bone. To do that was also my employment for several days until the bone [was] completely polished, and my jaws wearied and sore so that I feared lock jaw would ensue. The prowling of the wolves, and their howling in the sugar loaf mountains, about twenty-five miles distant, I could hear very distinctly, but they never came very near me.

But hunger, hunger increased its torments, so that I was compelled to go in search of food. I got weaker, and lay about where logs or any slight concealment was to be had, and I listened to any sounds which might bespeak human habitation. One morning, thus listening, I heard a voice speaking to the horse ploughing, and going towards the spot from where the sound proceeded I came up to a fence, looked over and saw newly ploughed ground, and I knew the person ploughing would soon come along. I waited in anxious suspense to speak to the person of whose kindness I was so deplorably in need. In a while I was gratified by the sight of this young female slave. I called her by name, she was frightened, and she then told me how bad I looked. I begged of her to give me a morsel of bread. She said my master had been round and requested the people not to give or allow their slaves to give me anything to eat, for if I could not get across the Ohio river I should be starved into giving myself up, and he would put a thousand lashes on me, and she cried, and I cried. I continued to beg a bit from her and at last she said she would try to get some for me. When she returned from dinner, she brought me a piece of bread about two ounces; she brought it away carefully and concealed it in her bosom, knowing that detection would ensure her a whipping. When she handed it over to me I felt how! what! I can scarcely say, I was so grateful.

I have spoken of hunger, hunger was not now uppermost in my thoughts. The river, can I cross it? Shall I be able after all to get away? Shall I reach Canada, the land of the free? Shall I, can I, escape the thousand lashes? They will torment me unto death if I am caught. I had little counsel, no directions how to proceed or where to go from my friend, but away again for the swamp, with a miserable feeling over my bread. I tried to keep up my spirits for the future, and perform my escape. I got back to my old holt under the rocks with a bare crumb left of my previous morsel, but it was finished, all gone before morning. Having eaten it so sparingly doubtless made it more useful than it otherwise would have been, but the next morning I was only the more hungry than before. What could be my thoughts now, reader? Bears, wolves, snakes, the very berries to which I had recourse for a meal, although my stomach would often reject them, might prove instruments of death! I felt this, and above all the thought that I might have to go into slavery again almost dejected and perplexed me, and yet I was much engaged in prayer, and enjoyed a peaceful calm, which none but him that feels it knows, a peace which knows no earthly sorrow, it came from the poor sinner's friend. I felt that only God's care over me had preserved me in life so many days in the wilderness waste.

One day as I sat about I espied a mink, a small black animal, as much like a weasel as any thing I know in England, and about the size of a half-grown domestic cat. It prowls on the chickens in the poultry yards; it is never eaten only in extreme cases. I watched it for an hour and a half like a cat watching for a mouse, but as I stealthily drew near it by drawing myself along the ground, he returned to the water and disappointed me of my anticipated repast. Night came on; oppressed, you may suppose, in body and mind, I issued forth to see what I could procure. I heard the sound of geese, I followed the sound, and coming to a fence I looked over a yard. By a house I saw a dog lying down which I took for a goose in the darkness of the night. I made up to it as quietly as I could, fearing to alarm the inmates, and [upon] putting my arms around it he ran off barking. I hastened from the spot for about twenty yards when a musket shot was fired at me; the shot seemed to whistle over my head. [To] being bent down by weakness I attribute my escape; had I stood upright my life had been taken. Even this, reader, was a token of the protecting Providence which has ever been sheltering the wandering son of affliction. I retreated once more to my old haunt to make my bed among the vipers, &c., who were destined to become my refuge, more merciful to me than man, fellow man, who sought my life, hunted down by them as the beasts of the forest. The two nights stern hunger drove me again to seek food. I hastened on, but finding nothing I lay beside a log and oppressed nature gave way; I fell asleep trusting in the arms of the omnipotent. I awoke just before the break of day hearing the bark of a dog. I traced the ground and came to a [h]ollow, a place [w]here the ground is cleared. The stumps in many instances being four feet from the ground, I crept from one stump to another to within a hundred yards of the house. Hiding behind one of the largest, thinking whether I had better go to the door to beg food or not, fearing detection I lay down, as I could not bare [sic] the idea of being sent back to a cruel relentless master; death was preferable. I flew to prayer, the only place of safety, for it was my only desire to commune with Him who was able to receive the weary and heavy laden, and who could and formerly has set the captive free. Bound in body and soul, He has been to me a double deliverer; I will praise him while health is lent. I wrestled with God in prayer, simply casting myself upon Him for life or death! Mark, the answering God of Jacob, the same yesterday, to-day, and for ever, he heard and listened. To his answer I raised my sorrowful face, and beheld a woman bearing an Indian basket made of splints. She went towards her oven, situated over a hundred yards from the house; she passed me unobserved, and I saw her fill it with bread. She carried away the basket of bread. I stole out of my hiding place, and on gaining the oven I looked in, perchance to find a crumb, when, oh! the indescribable joy I felt; one loaf was left! I snatched at it, and creeping as before with my new found treasure, biting it as I proceeded, regained my stump. Not long after she returned, and finding the loaf gone, for her basket would hold no more, she fled towards the house. I staggered off by degrees until I gained the bush where I ate some of the bread, and then fearful of being sought for, I, as well as I was able, returned to the swamp. In this noisome place I knelt and returned thanks to my Saviour for this token of his love. Surely, even at this moment of privation, I was rich; nor would I exchange places with my tyrannical persecutor, whose god is of this world and whose end is destruction. I must here remark that when the woman came back for the loaf, without the basket, and finding the loaf gone, I think I never saw a human being run so before; it was more like flying into the house, which gave me time to get to the bush. The bread which I could have eaten up all at once I made last me over a day. After that was finished, I gave myself up to die; I could see no other escape from hateful slavery. Did I ever think to enjoy such an unspeakable privilege as the present in bondage[?] I thought among the beasts and reptiles that surrounded me not one of them was half so frightful to me as the face of a white man. I feared to meet one lest he was sent to take me captive.

I thought amidst so many other things of a Mr. Wm. Brush, a Methodist preacher, who I would ask to become a mediator between my master and his slave. I applied to him, but he knew me only by my voice, I was so greatly altered. I was taken in by him and a cup of tea was given me by Mrs. Brush. Mr. Brush would not allow me to eat anything as he was fearful of killing me, he said, and the charge would be laid to him. I was at the distance of nineteen miles from the house of my master, to whom Mr. Brush consented to take me provided I promised to kneel at my master's feet and sue for pardon, to crave pardon for attempting to breathe the free air of liberty. And how shall I describe, reader, the fearful feelings that took possession of me as I neared the abode of my tyrant master[?]

[E]maciated and sick with fear, and within a quarter of a mile from my master's house, I could have sunk with dread knowing the revengeful heart of my master, who I knew had promised me 1000 lashes. Mr. Brush bade me stand at the door while he went in. He told my master he had brought his man Francis back home. "Have you," said he, "then I will cut the back of him to pieces." I thought I should have sunk and my heart died within me at the sound. Mr. Brush said, "I have promised him that you will not whip him." "Well," he said, "for your sake I will not." My kind mistress came crying to me saying, "Oh! Francis, is this you? Is it possible it's you?" I answered, "Oh! mistress, I have long desired to see you, that you might speak a kind word for me." My mistress took me in charge to feed me a little at a time that I might not kill myself by over eating. For the space of ten days I was frightful to behold; after nine weeks being in the swamp half starved, I was merely a living skeleton. After three weeks from the time Mr. Brush delivered me up he soon forgot the promise he had made by giving me 107 lashes with a cow hide. Though I had a cruel master, I had a kind mistress whom I loved; she tried to prevail upon her husband not to flog me, but no persuasion could prevent his blood-thirsty purpose. "He has been gone nine weeks and whip him I will." And any of the slaves when they are ready for the whip, the master flogs them himself. Those who can come and lay their soft hands on the shoulders of their husbands saying, "Do not make a fool of yourself, come into the house and leave this place!" Oh! how I wished my beloved mistress had this influence over her husband, but she had not.

After my severe flogging I was taken into the kitchen again to instruct the girl who had to cook during the nine weeks I was away until I recovered from my stripes; it was about two months before I was able to do anything, and then I was to take to my cooking again. I should have got on very well could I have kept my master from the kitchen; a great many times when he was on the spree, as we termed his drunken fits, he made me hold my hands down to my sides, his revolver sticking in his side pocket for me to see, while he would kick me and slap my face, [I] not daring to raise my hand in self defense for fear he would put his threat into execution and shoot me. He would then go into the spinning rooms and whip the women who were spinning there; then he would go out into the fields and whip them there. Coming back from the fields to the house he would meet a fat pig in the path and rub him on the back and play with him. Meeting with the dog he would play with him with the same kindness, calling him master's dog, and shake him as though he was his own child. He was accustomed to feed and treat the animals with greater kindness than he would treat me, for when on meeting me as he entered the kitchen he would fly at me as a lion would at a horse, striking me he cared not where, striking me on my face, eyes, or head, so that it caused me to wish many a time that I was a pig or a dog for I saw they were treated with more kindness than a slave, and I have wondered with you, dear reader, since I have been more enlightened, why I should have so wished it. When all the reward I had after a day's toil was hard words and cruel blows, it levels man with the beast, and blunts his finer feelings. But when the sweet soothing voice of Jesus whispers consolation, then it takes part of this heavy load and restores the poor slave to his former position as one of God's creation, made after his own image, a little lower than the angels.

A short time ago I was struck by an incident that occurred at Camelford, in Cornwall; a man who for whipping his horse was fined L.4. Surely, thought I, a man may be whipped to death in slavery unpitied and unknown, but even a horse may not receive unjust treatment without a punishment. This is a credit to England! And this I saw since I came to these shores. When I issued forth from bondage to a land of freedom it was like stepping from death into life, from the deepest shades of night into the glorious sunny realms of liberty! Liberty! What charms in that sound. Received by kind friends who were not ashamed to call me brother, who knew that skins may differ, yet affection dwells in white as well as black the same.

Coming into the kitchen one morning my master used me with such violence and severity that I ran out of the kitchen. My presumption in quitting the room so enraged him that he told me I should not enter it again. Accordingly, I was compelled to work in the fields in the cold month of January, to husk Indian corn. A slave being used to the warmth and comforts of a cooking kitchen as I was, being cook, such a sudden transit from heat to cold caused my hands to be crippled so much that I could not work as I formerly did. My being frost bitten, my feet being also much wounded, and being so ill used and crippled, and of no use to my master, he therefore tried to sell me to a Negro trader, but he would not have me, my limbs were too disabled for him to speculate by buying me. This made my master more hardened towards me, and the trader took it as an insult in offering him such useless property as he said I was. My master took out his revolver and said he had a good mind to blow my brains out. The next time he was tipsy, he, having heard I had been to a prayer meeting on the night I speak of, was so enraged that he gave me 215 lashes. Reader, you may wonder at me giving an account of the number of lashes I received, but when any of the slaves were whipped those who stood by used to count them and tell it to the one who had received the lashes. This so enfeebled me I thought I never should live after it. Two weeks after this, or less I think, I delivered myself into the hands of friends who came to my help. Raised up by my God, this kind friend who was a neighbour of my master's, I told him of the ill usage and my sufferings. He was very kind and he told me to come one Friday night, with no clothes or anything else but what I wore, and he would let me ride in his wagon to Mazewell [Maysville] from the power of my cruel master, whose heart was blacker than the veriest black African that I had ever seen.

The general Assembly of the North and South admit that slavery is innocent, but I can see no innocence in a slave holder ordering a fellow man 215 lashes for trying to serve his God. I felt now determined to give my cruel master leg bail, and I think it is innocence of heart for me to strive for liberty as ever it is for him to deprive me of it. It was very hard for me to leave my poor aged mother and five sisters behind me in slavery, and [it] was days and weeks before I could get the better of it. I was put across the river Ohio by kind friends, and got on the Under Ground Railway. I came on for 160 miles to the Under Ground Station, and was then cured from the effects of the flogging. There were two kind children of the names of John and Charlotte; John was twelve and Charlotte ten years of age. You will excuse me not giving the names of these children more explicit; to expose it would prevent others from helping a poor slave out of captivity, and we never do expose their real names. After I was cured of the flogging these children seemed to take a great interest in me. Johnny asked me if I could spell. I said no! Can you read? No, I said. Charlotte asked me the same questions and I told her the same as I told her brother. They said I should learn, and I told them I was too old. Oh, said they, you are not too old. Still I said I was. Johnny opened his spelling book and pointing to a letter said he, can you see that? And I said yes, and they laughed and said you can learn if you can see, and Johnny made me commence upon the alphabet, and with his instruction I said it over and over for 100 times until I had learnt it by heart. Johnny then learnt me the first syllable, and Charlotte the second. They then put me to learning the first of St. John's Gospel, and did not cease instructing me until I could read it. They then fetched their papa and mamma to hear me read it to them. They were glad and so was I, and very thankful too. I do not know which was the most pleased at heart, they or I. I then sung one of the slave hymns to them, and the family knelt down and I offered my prayers for them as they did not despise my black face, thanking God that he had brought me to such Christian people. I remained with them from November until the first of May, and it will never be effaced from my memory, the unbounded kindness I had met with from them, especially the two children who first taught me to read. Those children have been the cause of me loving children more than ever I had before; if I am with children at any time, and to hear them read, makes me feel like a child myself.

I left these christian people on the first of May, and arrived at Syndusky [Sandusky] City, and was put on board a boat, and came across lake Erie into Mishigan [*sic*]. And I then took the Under Ground Railway again, came on to York State. From York State to lake Ontario I took a steamer for Upper Canada. When I was safe landed in Upper Canada I shall never forget how I jumped and skipped about when I was told my master could not take me again into slavery.

I cannot say it was unfortunate, but I can say it was very fortunate for me, for I married an Englishwoman, who was a native of Devonshire, a widow, and had been so for five years previous to my marrying her. We then started from Toronto to England, and arrived in Liverpool on the 27th of August, 1857, and I have made my home principally in Plymouth. I cannot express my feelings at the kindness I have received since I landed in England from the English towards a coloured man, such is the difference between this country and America.

Reader, it is and ever will be my pride and delight to live a man of integrity, as becomes a christian in every deed. May it be said of me as of one of old, a christian in whom there was no guile:—

I have escaped through countless dangers,
From the man who claimed my soul,
Mind, and body as his chattel,
Subject to his control.

Now I have come across the British ocean,
Here in England is my home;
As to those who still in bondage,
Brethren unto thee I come.

TESTIMONIALS

I hearby certify that having taken considerable pains to satisfy myself that the bearer, Francis Fedric, is a true man, and his case worthy of public sympathy, I have no hesitation whatever in most cordially and earnestly recommending him to the confidence and liberality of all. His character, too, has been carefully observed during twelvemonth's residence in this town, and has not failed to secure the esteem of all who have known him. His public lectures are *speaking facts* rather than prepared lectures, and are both interesting and calculated to awaken sympathy in behalf of the victims of Slavery. He is a *Christian* man, and therefore has a still higher claim upon the sympathy and aid of Christian people.

W. R. Noble
Minister of the Presbyterian Chapel, Plymouth
January 17, 1859.

———

I most sincerely concur in the foregoing testimony, and commend Francis Fedric to the sympathy and aid of Christian people in every place he may visit.

Aspinall Hampson
Minister of Prince's Street Chapel, Devonport.

———

It affords me much pleasure to state that the foregoing testimonials are fully borne out in the character and conduct of Francis Fedric, and from all I have seen of him since March last, I have every reason to believe him to be a christian man—one whose case I can cheerfully commend to the sympathy of the Christian public. I may also add he is an entire abstainer from intoxicating liquors of twenty-three years' standing.

> Wm. Rose
> Minister of Gideon Chapel, Newfoundland Street,
> Bristol
> June 23, 1859.

F.F. also has testimonials from the following gentlemen:—

Mr. Thomas Binyon, of Manchester.
Rev. Franklin Haworth, Bury. Lancashire.
Mr. John Predeaux, Plymouth.
Rev. W. B. Jenkyn, Minister of the Wycliffe Chapel, Bristol.
Dr. Morton Brown, Cheltenham.
Mr. Lewis B. Jones, Burslem, Staffordshire.

BIBLIOGRAPHY

Allen, William. G. *The American Prejudice Against Color: An Authentic Narrative, Showing how Easily the Nation Got into an Uproar.* London: W. and F. G. Cash, 1853.

Bhabha, Homi K. *The Location of Culture.* London: Routledge, 1994.

Bibb, Henry. *Narrative of the Life and Adventures of Henry Bibb, an American Slave.* New York: Negro Universities Press, 1969.

Blackett, R. J .M. *Building an Antislavery Wall: Black Americans in the Atlantic Abolitionist Movement, 1830–1860.* Baton Rouge: Louisiana State University Press, 1983.

———. "Cracks in the Anti-Slavery Wall." In *Liberating Sojourn: Frederick Douglass and Transatlantic Reform,* ed. Alan J. Rice and Martin Crawford. Athens: University of Georgia Press, 1999.

———, ed. *Running a Thousand Miles for Freedom: The Escape of William and Ellen Craft from Slavery.* Baton Rouge: Louisiana State University Press, 1999.

Blassingame, John W.. *The Slave Community: Plantation Life in the Antebellum South.* New York: Oxford University Press, 1972.

Blunt, Reginald. *Memoirs of Gerald Blunt of Chelsea.* London: Printed for the author, 1911.

Bolt, Christine. *The Anti-Slavery Movement and Reconstruction: A Study in Anglo-American Co-operation, 1833–77.* London: Oxford University Press, 1969.

———. *Victorian Attitudes to Race.* London: Routledge, 1971.

Bolt, Christine, and Seymour Drescher, eds. *Anti-Slavery, Religion, and Reform: Essays in Memory of Roger Anstey.* Folkestone, U.K.: W. Dawson & Sons, 1980.

Bordewich, Fergus M. *Bound for Canaan: The Underground Railroad and the War for the Soul of America.* New York: Amistad, 2005.

Brady, E. A. "A Reconsideration of the Lancaster Cotton Famine." *Agricultural History* (July 1963): 156–62.

Brody, Jennifer De Vere. *Impossible Purities: Blackness, Femininity, and Victorian Culture.* Durham, N.C.: Duke University Press, 1998.

Brown, John. *Slave Life in Georgia: A Narrative of the Life, Sufferings, and Escape of John Brown, a Fugitive Slave, Now in England.* Ed. L. A. Chamerovzow. London: W. M. Watts, 1855.

Campbell, Madison. *The Autobiography of Elder Madison Campbell, Pastor of the United Colored Baptist Church, Richmond, Kentucky.* Richmond, Ky.: Pantagraph Job Rooms, 1895.

Coleman, J. Winston, Jr. "Lexington's Slave Dealers and Their Southern Trade." *Filson Club History Quarterly* 12 (1938).

Craft, William. *Running a Thousand Miles for Freedom; or, The Escape of William and Ellen Craft from Slavery.* 1860. Rpr. Baton Rouge: Louisiana State University Press, 1999.

Douglass, Frederick. *Narrative of the Life of Frederick Douglass, an American Slave: Written by Himself.* Ed. Houston A. Baker. Harmondsworth, U.K.: Penguin, 1982.

Drew, Benjamin. *The Refugee: A North-Side View of Slavery.* 1855. Reading, Mass.: Addison-Wesley, 1969.

Edwards, Paul, and David Dabydeen, eds. *Black Writers in Britain, 1760–1890.* Edinburgh: Edinburgh University Press, 1995.

Equiano, Olaudah. *The Interesting Narrative of the Life of Olaudah Equiano, or Gustavus Vassa, the African, Written by Himself.* Ed. Vincent Carretta. Harmondsworth, U.K.: Penguin, 1995.

Farnie, D. A. "The Cotton Famine in Great Britain." In *Great Britain and Her World, 1750–1914: Essays in Honour of W. O. Henderson,* ed. B. M. Ratcliffe. Manchester: Manchester University Press, 1975.

Fisch, Audrey. *American Slaves in Victorian England: Abolitionist Politics in Popular Literature and Culture.* Cambridge: Cambridge University Press, 2000.

Frost, Karolyn Smardz. *I've Got a Home in Glory Land: A Lost Tale of the Underground Railroad.* New York: Farrar, Straus & Giroux, 2007.

Fryer, Peter. *Staying Power: The History of Black People in Britain.* London: Pluto Press, 1984.

Gara, Larry. *The Liberty Line: The Legend of the Underground Railroad.* Lexington: University of Kentucky Press, 1961.

Gates, Henry Louis, Jr. *The Signifying Monkey: A Theory of Afro-American Literary Criticism.* New York: Oxford University Press, 1988.

———. "A Dangerous Literacy: The Legacy of Frederick Douglass." *New York Times Book Review,* May 28, 1995, 3.

Gikandi, Simon. *Maps of Englishness: Writing Identity in the Culture of Colonialism.* New York: Columbia University Press, 1996.

Gilroy, Paul. *The Black Atlantic: Modernity and Double Consciousness.* Cambridge, Mass.: Harvard University Press, 1993.

Griffler, Keith P. *Front Line of Freedom: African Americans and the Forging of the Underground Railroad in the Ohio Valley.* Lexington: University Press of Kentucky, 2004.

Hagedorn, Ann. *Beyond the River: The Untold Story of the Heroes of the Underground Railroad.* New York: Simon & Schuster, 2002.

Hall, Catherine. *White, Male, and Middle-Class: Explorations in Feminism and History.* Cambridge: Polity Press, 1992.

Hall, Stuart. "Cultural Identity and Diaspora." In *Colonial Discourse and Postcolonial Theory: A Reader,* ed. Patrick Williams and Laura Chrisman. Hemel Hampstead, U.K.: Harvester Wheatsheaf, 1993. 392–403.

Harrison, Lowell H. *The Antislavery Movement in Kentucky.* Lexington: University Press of Kentucky, 1978.

Hedrick, Charles E. "Negro Slavery in Kentucky Before 1850." M.A. thesis, University of Chicago, 1915.

Henderson, W. O. *The Lancashire Cotton Famine, 1861–1865.* Manchester: Manchester University Press, 1934.

Henson, Josiah. *An Autobiography of Rev. Josiah Henson (Mrs. H. Beecher Stowe's "Uncle Tom").* Ed. J. Lobb. London: Christian Age, 1890.

Hudson, J. Blaine. *Fugitive Slaves and the Underground Railroad in the Kentucky Borderland.* Jefferson, N.C.: McFarlane & Co., 2002.

Innes, C. L. *A History of Black and Asian Writing in Britain.* 2nd ed. Cambridge: Cambridge University Press, 2008.

Johnson, Thomas L. *Twenty-Eight Years a Slave; or, The Story of My Life in Three Continents.* Bournemouth, U.K.: W. Mate and Sons, 1909. (Shorter version first published in 1882.)

Landon, Fred. "The Negro Migration to Canada after the Passing of the Fugitive Slave Act." *Journal of Negro History* 5 (January 1920): 22–36.

Lorimer, Douglas A. *Colour, Class, and the Victorians: English Attitudes to the*

Negro in the Mid-Nineteenth Century. Leicester, U.K.: Leicester University Press, 1978.

Lucas, Marion B. *A History of Blacks in Kentucky,* vol. 1. Frankfort: Kentucky Historical Society, 1992.

Marsh, Jan, ed. *Black Victorians: Black People in British Art, 1800–1900.* Aldershot: Lund Humphries, 2005.

Martin, Asa Earl. *The Anti-slavery Movement in Kentucky, Prior to 1850.* Louisville: Standard Printing Co., 1918.

Meer, Sarah. *Uncle Tom Mania: Slavery, Minstrelsy, and Transatlantic Culture in the 1850s.* Athens: University of Georgia Press, 2005.

Midgley, Clare. *Women Against Slavery: The British Campaign, 1780–1870.* London: Routledge, 1992.

Noonan, Barry Christopher. *Blacks in Canada, 1861.* Madison, Wisc.: B. Noonan, 2000.

Owens, Leslie Howard. *This Species of Property: Slave Life and Culture in the Old South.* New York: Oxford University Press, 1976.

Pemberton, Ian. "The Anti-Slavery Society of Canada." M.A. thesis, University of Toronto, 1967.

Quarles, Benjamin. *Black Abolitionists.* New York: Oxford University Press, 1969.

Ripley, C. Peter, ed. *The Black Abolitionist Papers, Vol. I: The British Isles, 1830–1865.* Chapel Hill: University of North Carolina Press, 1985.

————. *The Black Abolitionist Papers, Vol. II: Canada, 1830–1865.* Chapel Hill: University of North Carolina Press, 1985.

Roper, Moses. *A Narrative of the Adventures and Escape of Moses Roper, from American Slavery.* London: Darton, Harvey, and Darton, 1837.

Siebert, Wilbur. *The Underground Railroad from Slavery to Freedom.* New York: Macmillan, 1898.

Smith, Harry. *Fifty Years in Slavery in the United States of America.* Grand Rapids: West Michigan Printing Co., 1891.

Sprague, Stuart Seely, ed. *His Promised Land: The Autobiography of John P. Parker, Former Slave and Conductor on the Underground Railroad.* New York: Norton, 1996.

Stanford, Peter. *From Bondage to Liberty.* London: Smethwick, 1889.

Stuckey, Sterling. *Slave Culture: Nationalist Theory and the Foundations of Black America.* New York: Oxford University Press, 1987.

Temperley, Howard. *British Antislavery, 1833–1870.* London: Longman, 1972.

Turley, David. *The Culture of English Antislavery, 1780–1860.* London: Routledge, 1991.

Walvin, James, comp. *The Black Presence: A Documentary History of the Negro in England, 1555–1860.* London: Orbach and Chambers, 1971.

————. *Black and White: The Negro and English Society, 1555–1945.* Harmondsworth: Penguin, 1973.

Ward, Samuel Ringgold. *Autobiography of a Fugitive Negro: His Anti-Slavery Labours in the United States, Canada, and England.* London: John Snow, 1855.

Waters, Hazel. "Putting on 'Uncle Tom' on the Victorian Stage," *Race and Class* 42, no. 3 (January–March 2001): 29–48.

Winks, Robin W. *The Blacks in Canada: A History.* New Haven: Yale University Press, 1971.

INDEX